Early Christians

To F. F. Bruce
Christian, mentor and friend

Early Christians

John W. Drane

1817

HARPER & ROW, PUBLISHERS, SAN FRANCISCO
Cambridge, Hagerstown, New York, Philadelphia
London, Mexico City, São Paulo, Sydney

FIRST U.S. EDITION

ISBN 0–06–062067–6

82 83 84 85 10 9 8 7 6 5 4 3 2 1

Printed in Great Britain

The photographs in this book are reproduced by permission of the following photographers and organizations:
Barnaby's Picture Library: 21, 33, 49, 53, 60, 73, 81, 87, 110 and 111, 131; Juliette Radom 13, 38, 84, 99.
British Museum: 79, 92, 130.
Church Missionary Society: 138 and 139.
Keith Ellis: 67.
Gordon Gray: 17.
Sonia Halliday Photographs: F. H. C. Birch 40 and 41; Sonia Halliday 10, 23, 30 and 31, 36, 119; Jane Taylor 32, 94 and 95, 104, 107, 112.
Lion Publishing: David Alexander 16, 25, 31, 39, 45, 70, 90 and 91, 127, 135.
Ake Lundberg: 57.
Mansell Collection: 19, 24, 46 (both), 47, 51, 54, 56, 85, 124.
Open Doors: 101.
Ivor Philip: 140.
Picturepoint: 113.
Popperfoto: 72.
Clifford Shirley: 64, 65, 75.
Topham: 128 and 129.
World Vision International: 134.
Wycliffe Bible Translators: 35.

Maps by Roy Lawrance and Lesley Passey.

Contents

Continued over

Chapter 3. The church and its Jewish origins

Chapter 4. The enemies within

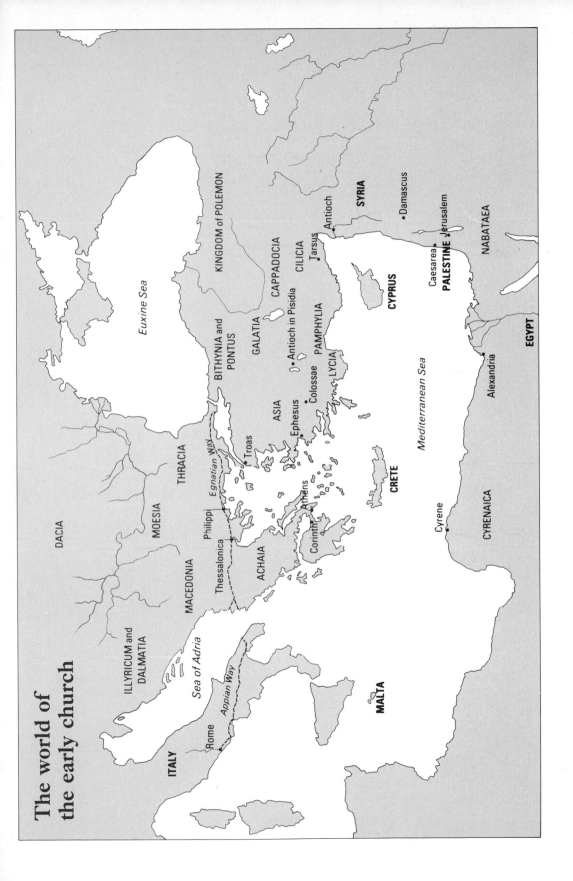

The world of
the early church

ITALY

Rome

Appian Way

Sea of Adria

ILLYRICUM and DALMATIA

DACIA

MOESIA

THRACIA

MACEDONIA

Philippi

Thessalonica

Egnatian Way

ACHAIA

Corinth

Athens

Troas

Euxine Sea

KINGDOM of POLEMON

BITHYNIA and PONTUS

GALATIA

CAPPADOCIA

ASIA

Ephesus

Colossae

Antioch in Pisidia

PAMPHYLIA

LYCIA

CILICIA

Tarsus

Antioch

SYRIA

Damascus

Jerusalem

Caesarea

PALESTINE

NABATAEA

CYPRUS

Mediterranean Sea

CRETE

MALTA

Cyrene

CYRENAICA

Alexandria

EGYPT

1 Confronting the ancient world

THE LIFE of the early church began with the life of just one remarkable person, Jesus of Nazareth. He was born about 4 BC into an ordinary working-class Jewish family, and as a young man he made a name for himself as a religious teacher. Indeed, though he was in the public gaze for little more than three years before his life was tragically cut short by his execution on a Roman cross, in that short time he delivered a message about God that was to exert a crucial influence not only on his own people, but on the subsequent course of world history.

No doubt his appearance was not all that remarkable in the context of the Palestinian countryside where he lived and worked. After all, the Jewish religion had many hundreds of wandering teachers, or 'rabbis' as they were called – men of exceptional gift and insight who would gather round them small groups of disciples to perpetuate their teachings after they were gone. The stories

Matthew 2:1; Luke 2:1-7

Luke 23:33

The Sea of Galilee was the scene of much of Jesus' teaching and healing, and some of his first disciples were fishermen.

Matthew 10:1-4
Mark 6:30-44; 8:1-9
about Jesus in the New Testament Gospels tell us how he himself had twelve special followers, though they also report that on more than one occasion thousands of people flocked to hear his teaching. But what really sets Jesus apart from the other rabbis is the fact that it was not on the shores of the inland Sea of Galilee among simple Jewish peasants that his teaching made its greatest impact. For in a very short time after his death, his personality and his beliefs were having a profound effect in places far removed from the shores of Palestine.

Spread of the new faith

Acts 8:26-39

Within twenty years or less of his crucifixion, every major centre of civilization round the Mediterranean Sea could boast at least one group of his followers. The New Testament reports the existence of Christians in Rome, Corinth, Ephesus, Philippi, Antioch in Syria, and many other Roman cities – not to mention its cryptic reports of Christians from places such as Alexandria in Egypt, or Ethiopia, or Byzantium. This is not all that surprising when it is realized that the list of people present in Jerusalem to hear Peter's first public sermon reads like a roll-call of most of the cities in the ancient world: 'We are from Parthia, Media, and Elam; from Mesopotamia, Judea, and Cappadocia; from Pontus and Asia, from Phrygia and Pamphylia, from Egypt and the regions of Libya near Cyrene. Some of us are from Rome, both Jews and Gentiles converted to Judaism,

Acts 2:9-11
and some of us are from Crete and Arabia . . .' Presumably not all of them became Christians. But many of them did, and it was not long before these new disciples of Jesus began to exert an increasingly powerful influence on life even in Rome itself.

Writing of events in AD 49, less than twenty years after the death of Jesus, the Roman historian Suetonius describes a series of riots that led the emperor Claudius to expel the Jewish population from
Life of Claudius 25.4
the city. And according to him, the cause of all the trouble was a person whom he calls 'Chrestus'. Scholars have debated the precise identity of this person, but there seems little doubt that the events Suetonius records were brought about by arguments over the teaching of those Jews who had become followers of Jesus the Messiah (Latin *Christus*).

Opposition

Origen, *Against Celsus* 8.17; 3.14;
Minucius Felix, *Octavius* 8.4; 9.1-6

It was not long before the popular press of the Roman world turned their attention to these followers of Jesus: 'The Christians form among themselves secret societies that exist outside the system of laws . . . an obscure and mysterious community founded on revolt and on the advantage that accrues from it . . . They form a rabble of profane conspiracy. Their alliance consists in meetings at night with solemn rituals and inhuman revelries . . . They despise temples as if they were tombs. They disparage the gods and ridicule our sacred rites . . . Just like a rank growth of weeds, the abominable haunts where this impious confederacy meet are multiplying all over the world . . . To venerate an executed criminal and . . . the wooden cross on which he was executed is to erect altars which befit lost and depraved wretches.'

Acts 2:32

Acts 12:1-5; 2 Corinthians 11:23-27

Not that the Christians themselves would have agreed with any of this. For, far from worshipping 'an executed criminal', these men and women who were causing such social upheaval firmly believed that their Jesus was not dead, but was really and truly alive, and was with them wherever they went. This was the one crucial factor which ensured the lasting success of the whole Christian enterprise. Because they believed that Jesus was not dead, but alive, his first followers were prepared to take the most incredible risks in spreading their message. Beatings, imprisonments, shipwrecks, and persecutions of all kinds – even death – were commonplace in the life of the early churches. And the results were spectacular.

Of course, we look back on all this with the wisdom of hindsight. We know that the church did in fact succeed. But if we put ourselves in the position of those first followers of Jesus, we can see that their success was by no means a foregone conclusion. Indeed, quite the opposite. By normal standards everything was against them. Jesus himself was a Jew, as were all his original disciples – and though in some circles in the Roman Empire the Jewish religion was respected, on the whole the Jews living in Palestine were regarded as an incomprehensible, fanatical and unbalanced race. On top of that, neither Jesus nor his followers were of high social standing. They came from the backwoods of rural Palestine. It must have been hard enough for them to gain a hearing even in their own local religious capital, Jerusalem – not to mention the problems of communicating with educated Greeks and Romans in the wider world outside. Yet this is precisely what they did, as a movement that began spontaneously in a country on the edge of Roman civilization suddenly became an important social and political, as well as religious force at the very centre of life in the empire.

So what was their secret? Why did these people feel impelled to take the message of Jesus to the furthest corners of the world they knew? Why did they not instead stay at home, to become a reforming movement within the Jewish religion they all knew? To understand the answers to these questions, we must briefly go back to the very beginning of the story, to the life and teaching of Jesus himself.

In the beginning

Mark 1:21; Luke 4:16

In many respects Jesus' activities were not all that different from other Jewish teachers of the time. Like other rabbis, he travelled from place to place with his message, and took time to speak to people wherever he happened to meet them. Sometimes it was in religious meetings at the local Jewish place of worship (the synagogue). At other times he spoke to them in the street, or out in the fields, or at their places of work. Like other rabbis, Jesus had his followers – hundreds, or even thousands of people who had a general interest in what he was saying, together with a smaller group of more immediate disciples who were being trained to continue his mission after him.

Luke 9:25; 19:18,39

So it is not surprising that the people who met Jesus generally recognized him as a rabbi, and gave him that title. Most of these other religious teachers in the Jewish religion had themselves been disciples of other rabbis. They had grown up in the system, and their teaching owed a great deal to their own predecessors. But right from the very beginning, people recognized that Jesus was different, and that his message was distinctive. Mark sets the scene in his very first report of Jesus' public teaching: 'The people who heard him were amazed at the way he taught, for he wasn't like the teachers of the Law; instead, he taught with authority.'

Mark 1:22

That does not mean to say that his teaching was completely new and unique. Many Jewish writers have rightly pointed out that almost everything in Jesus' teaching had been said before him by the Jewish rabbis. Since both Jesus and the rabbis were setting out to explain the significance of the Old Testament for their own generation, it is hardly surprising that they sometimes reached the same conclusions. But what was so different about Jesus – and what

The Law still has great significance for the orthodox Jew. Here a rabbi holds the Sefer Torah, or scroll of the Law.

was to set his followers radically apart from Judaism – was the framework in which he set his teaching. For on two basic issues Jesus adopted a fundamentally different stance from the other Jewish teachers of his day.

Keeping the law
Genesis – Deuteronomy

The Law, or Torah (the first five books of the Old Testament), was central to the Jewish faith. By keeping the Law in all its details a person demonstrated his or her obedience and faithful response to God. It is often difficult for a non-Jew today to understand the almost mystical significance of the Law for a faithful Jewish believer in the time of Jesus. For instance, it has been shown recently that some of the most influential Protestant biblical scholars of the last 100 years or so have been guilty of a gross misrepresentation of the Jewish attitude to law-keeping. Judaism was not the rigid, legalistic system that many people imagine. Pious Jews in the time of Jesus must have had a far more positive understanding of their faith than the kind of blind obedience credited to them by some Christian writers in modern times. But no matter what their motivation, keeping the Law and its precepts has always been a central plank of Judaism. To be a good person, one must keep the Law.

But there was more than one way to do that. As long as 700 years before the time of Jesus, the prophet Amos had condemned his contemporaries for their eagerness to keep the minute details of the ritual and ceremonial regulations, while ignoring the central moral requirements that were also laid down in the Torah. And things were no different in Jesus' day. His condemnation of the Pharisees, one of the leading religious groups of the day, is strongly reminiscent of Amos's warnings: 'You hypocrites! You give to God a tenth even of the seasoning herbs, such as mint, dill, and cumin, but you neglect to obey the really important teachings of the Law, such as justice and mercy and honesty.' The problem was obviously widespread, for when Jesus was asked why his disciples did not keep every detailed requirement of the Old Testament Law, he pointed out to his questioners their own inconsistency in avoiding moral obligations to their parents by using a legal loophole to use their wealth for more 'religious' purposes. 'And', added Jesus, 'there are many other things like this that you do.'

Jesus never denied the validity of the Old Testament Law, nor did he deny that it had been given by God. But he did suggest that with his own coming, its day was finished. More than that, in a series of remarkable statements he contrasts his own teaching with that of the Torah, and elevates his own authority to a higher status than that of Moses, the great Old Testament law-giver: 'You have heard that people were told in the past [by Moses] but now I tell you . . .' It is also significant that according to Mark's account of his trial before the Sanhedrin, Jesus was first charged with blasphemy against the temple. The charge failed, but from the authorities' viewpoint it was not totally without foundation, as we can see from his statement in Matthew's Gospel: 'I tell you that there is something here greater than the temple.'

Amos 5:21-24

Matthew 23:23

Mark 7:1-13

Luke 16:16

Matthew 5:21-22, 27-28, 31-47

Mark 14:57-59

Matthew 12:6

It is therefore not surprising that, though Jesus seemed to be an ordinary Jewish rabbi, he was soon outlawed by the Jewish religious establishment. This radical teaching about the Law and the temple was striking at the very foundations of their most firmly-held convictions. Of course, many rabbis had asked awkward questions before – and if Jesus' teaching had been restricted to theoretical debate about the Law, perhaps the system could have coped with it. It had survived many changes before, and was to assimilate many others after the time of Jesus. But Jesus was not content to be just a propounder of theories, and the way he behaved was, if anything, even more scandalous than his teaching.

Mark tells how he and his disciples disregarded the Jewish laws about the sabbath day, picking grain as they walked through the fields – actions that were regarded as harvesting by pious believers. Jesus' reply to the Pharisees' criticism of this behaviour was to dismiss their concern for the keeping of the Law with the declaration that 'The Sabbath was made for the good of man; man was not made for the Sabbath'. Then when he was asked why his disciples disregarded the regulations about ritual washing before eating a meal, he dismissed the criticism by appeal to a higher principle: 'There is nothing that goes into a person from the outside which can make him ritually unclean. Rather, it is what comes out of a person that makes him unclean . . . evil ideas which lead him to do immoral things, to rob, kill, commit adultery, be greedy . . .'

Mark 2:23-28

Mark 7:1-15

Mark 7:21-22

In addition to all this, Jesus insisted on taking his message to all sorts of people who were regarded as unclean by pious Jews. Lepers, prostitutes, tax gatherers (Roman collaborators) – all of them figure prominently in the Gospels, and Jesus himself was described as 'a glutton and a drinker, a friend of tax collectors and other outcasts'. Instead of making his friends among the conventionally religious, Jesus chose those who were despised for their inability to keep the Law. Indeed, he made a virtue out of it, reminding his questioners on one occasion that 'I have not come to call respectable people, but outcasts'.

Matthew 11:19

Mark 2:17

A number of stories in the Gospels explain why Jesus felt like that, but perhaps none has a greater impact than the parable of the Pharisee and the tax collector who went to pray in the temple at the same time. The Pharisee prided himself on his moral and religious attainments – and told God so. The tax collector, on the other hand, was so conscious of his own unworthiness to speak to God at all that he could only cry out, 'God, have pity on me, a sinner'. 'But', said Jesus, 'the tax collector, and not the Pharisee, was in the right with God when he went home', because he recognized his own sinfulness and came to God with no spiritual pretensions.

Luke 18:9-14

The Pharisees were laying all the stress on external actions that could be assessed and regulated by rules. Jesus believed it was possible to keep all the rules, and yet not please God. And so in all his teaching, Jesus was much more concerned with what a person *is* than with what he or she *does*. Not that he believed actions to be unimportant. But Jesus realized that the way we behave depends on the kind of people we are. And for him, the secret of goodness was to be found not in obedience to rules, but in the spontaneous activities of a transformed character: 'A sound tree cannot bear evil fruit, nor can a bad tree bear good fruit.'

Matthew 7:18

Religion and race

But there was another element in Jesus' conflicts with the Jewish establishment. Many people in the Roman Empire admired the moral precepts of the Old Testament. The principles enshrined in the Ten Commandments and other parts of the Torah commanded the respect of many upright Romans and Greeks. But admiring the Law was not quite the same thing as pleasing God, and before they could be fully accepted as part of God's people, Jews demanded that non-Jews must be circumcised and be prepared to keep every detailed regulation of the Old Testament Law. In a word, they had to become Jews – for the Jewish people believed that they, and they alone, were the people of God, and others had no chance of being accepted by God unless they too accepted all the burdens of the Law. This did not stop the Pharisees and others from engaging in missionary activity among non-Jews. Indeed, Jesus himself commended them for their enthusiasm. But he did not approve of their insistence that in order to please God such people should accept all the detailed regulations of the Old Testament Law.

Matthew 23:15

The precise extent of Jesus' own involvement in a mission to those who were not Jews is somewhat unclear. He certainly made no concerted effort to preach the good news to non-Jews (Gentiles). But at the same time, all four Gospels show him accepting and respecting the faith of such people whenever he met them. He was not unwilling even to assist a Roman officer, remarking in the process that 'I have never found anyone in Israel with faith like this'.

Matthew 8:5-13

Jesus said that the way people live shows what they are really like, just as a healthy tree naturally produces good fruit.

Then a number of incidents show his acceptance of various foreign groups within Palestinian society, while one of his best-known parables extols the virtues of a Samaritan, the race that was despised perhaps more than any other by pious Jews.

Some readers of the Gospels have found a difficulty in Jesus' instruction to his disciples in Matthew 10:5-6, 'Do not go to any Gentile territory or any Samaritan towns. Instead, you are to go to those lost sheep, the people of Israel.' But this advice was given in respect of a limited mission tour which the disciples were to undertake for a short period only, during Jesus' own lifetime. Matthew himself certainly did not believe it to be binding advice for all time, for he is the only Gospel writer to record the great commission of Jesus, exhorting his disciples to 'Go . . . to all peoples everywhere and make them my disciples . . .' Other passages in Matthew's Gospel make the same point, as do many passages in the Gospel of Luke. The best way to understand the advice of Matthew 10:5 is to set it alongside another commission given, according to Luke, after the resurrection: '. . . you will be witnesses for me in Jerusalem, in all Judea and Samaria, and to the

Mark 5:1-20; 7:24-30

Luke 10:25-37

Matthew 28:19

Matthew 8:10-12; 21:43

Christians are actively involved in sharing their faith today in obedience to Jesus' command to be his witnesses.

Acts 1:8 ends of the earth'. For Jesus, evangelism, like charity, must begin a
home.

The church grows

It was one thing for the earliest followers of Jesus to have his
teaching and example on these matters, but quite another to pu'
them into practice. What had seemed in the context of Jesus' work
to be a simple, if radical approach to the traditions of Judaism and
the Old Testament was soon to emerge as the single most complex
issue with which the infant churches would have to wrestle. The
reasons for this, at least in the first instance, were social as much as
theological and religious.

During the lifetime of Jesus, the new Messianic movement which
he founded was for the most part a local sect in Palestinian Judaism.
All the disciples were Jews, and, though both the logic of Jesus'
message and the example of his own practice made it clear that
Gentiles were not to be excluded, the issue simply did not arise to
any great extent. Those Gentiles whom Jesus encountered himself
were isolated individuals. There were not many of them, and in any
case many of them were probably adherents in the local synagogues,
if not actual converts to Judaism.

Mark 7:24-30; Luke 7:1-10

But it was not long before the followers of Jesus were forced to
give considerable attention to the whole question of the relationship
between Jewish and Gentile believers. Though they did not realize
it at the time, the events of the Day of Pentecost recorded at the

The Roman Empire at its widest
extent in AD 117.

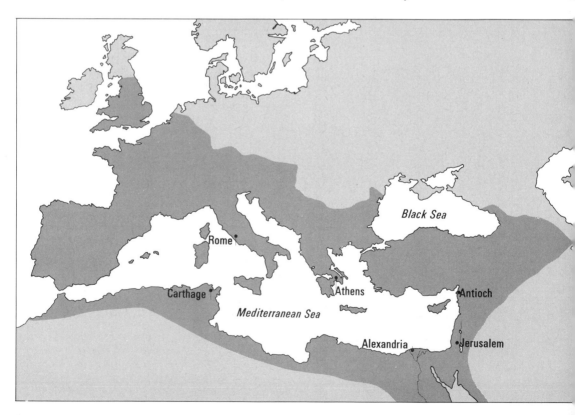

The Roman Empire at its widest extent in AD 117.

Acts 2

beginning of the book of Acts were to be a watershed in the life of the infant church. For when Peter stood up to explain the Christian message to the crowds in Jerusalem, he was facing a very cosmopolitan audience of 'religious men who had come from every country

Acts 2:5

of the world'. Naturally, they must all have been interested in Judaism, or they would not have travelled to Jerusalem for a religious festival. But not all the Gentiles among them would be full converts who had accepted the whole Jewish Law – while even those who were from Jewish families in various parts of the Roman Empire must have had a rather different background and outlook from those Jews who had been born and bred in Palestine itself.

Jews and Judaism in the Roman Empire

The Jewish 'diaspora', or dispersion, was crucial in forming beliefs and in the rise of the synagogue. Israelites were exiled to the city of Babylon in the time of Nebuchadnezzar. One of Babylon's many splendid buildings, the Ishtar Gate rose 50 feet/15 metres above a sacred processional way leading into the city.

Most of us today think of Palestine as the land of the Jews in New Testament times. But in fact there were probably more Jews living in a city like Alexandria in Egypt than there were in Jerusalem itself. Josephus quotes the Latin author Strabo, who said that the Jewish nation 'has already made its way into every city, and it is not easy to find any place in the habitable world which has not received this nation, and in which it has not made its power felt' (*Antiquities of the Jews* 14.7.2).

In Old Testament times, the land and people of Israel had been a self-contained geographical and national entity. Indeed, the Old Testament story is largely concerned with how Israel's ancestors had been gathered from various parts of the Middle East, to be united in their common heritage, the promised land of Canaan. But by the time of Jesus the process was working in reverse, and the Jewish people were living all over the world. This scattering, or 'Dispersion' as it is sometimes called, had begun many centuries before in 586 BC. That was the year when Nebuchadnezzar, king of Babylon, invaded the Old Testament kingdom of Judah. So that he could control the conquered nation, he took all the most gifted and influential inhabitants of Jerusalem off to a new life in Babylon. This was a disaster of immense proportions for the Jewish people. Politically, of course, it was the final catastrophe, for never again were the Jewish people to enjoy an independent existence. Yet in spite of that, this Jewish exile in Babylon was to become one of the most creative forces in the whole history of Jewish religion.

In the heyday of Old Testament religion, the worship of the temple in Jerusalem had been of central importance. It was by regular visits to the temple and the offering of sacrifices there that a person declared his loyalty to the God of Israel and his obedience to the Law. But Nebuchadnezzar destroyed the temple, and though the remnants of the population who were left in Jerusalem still continued to worship in its ruins, even that consolation was not possible for those who had been removed to Babylon. Their feelings were expressed most movingly in words from Psalm 137: 'By the rivers of Babylon we sat down; there we wept when we remembered Zion. On the willows near by we hung up our harps. Those who captured us told us to sing; they told us to entertain them: "Sing us a song about Zion". But how can we sing to the Lord in a foreign land? May I never be able to play the harp again if I forget you, O Jerusalem!'

In the event, Jerusalem was not forgotten, and it was not long before the exiles discovered that though at first it seemed inconceivable, they could indeed sing the Lord's songs in a foreign land. It was in the synagogue that they did so. In a different social setting, some things just had to be different, and the local synagogue was not a replica of the temple back in Jerusalem. Worship in Jerusalem had been concerned with sacrifices, but this was no longer possible, and in the worship at the synagogue the central place of sacrifice had to be filled by something else. So a form of worship developed which had no place for sacrifice. Instead, the emphasis was now laid on those things that Jews could do anywhere: prayer, the reading of the Torah, keeping the sabbath day, circumcision, and the observance of the Old Testament food laws.

This adaptation of traditional Jewish worship was so successful that when Jews from Babylon were eventually able to return to their homeland, they took it with them. And when, following the conquests of Alexander the Great (king of Macedon, 335–323 BC), other enterprising Jews decided to emigrate voluntarily to different parts of the Mediterranean world, it was natural that they should adopt the synagogue as the central expression of their religious and national allegiance. By the time the first Christian missionaries were beginning to travel the roads of the Roman Empire with the good news about Jesus, there was an extensive network of Jewish synagogues spread the length and breadth of the entire empire.

Not all synagogues were exactly the same, of course. In earlier times, the temple in Jerusalem had imposed a certain degree of central control over religious beliefs and practices – and it continued to do so in Palestine until its final destruction in AD 70. But the synagogues were much freer to develop their own ways of thinking. The problems of being a Jew in Babylon were quite different from the problems facing Jews in Rome, while the Egyptian city of Alexandria was different again. So in each local centre, Jewish people had to work out for themselves how best to face up to the challenges of their new environments. Even within the same locality, different synagogues could give different responses. In Rome, for example, some Jews were quite happy to go along with many aspects of pagan society, even giving their children Latin or Greek names, and adopting the art-forms of Roman civilization. But others in the same city deplored what they saw as a dilution and betrayal of their ancestral faith, and stuck rigidly to a more traditional understanding of the Old Testament Law.

We also know of Jews who became deeply interested in the study of Greek philosophy. The most famous of these was Philo, a Jew from the Egyptian city of Alexandria. We know few details of his life, but he must have been born some time before Jesus, and probably lived until the mid-forties of the first century AD. He was a member of an influential Jewish family, and some of his relatives became deeply involved in politics both in Egypt and elsewhere. But Philo was most interested in explaining the thinking of Greek writers, especially the Stoics. He found many of their ideas congenial, and set out to show how the Old Testament and Greek philosophy were really saying the same things in their own distinctive ways. In order to demonstrate this, he had to regard much of the Old Testament as a kind of allegorical or symbolic presentation of the truths expounded by the philosophers.

Orthodox Jews elsewhere in the empire would certainly have regarded Philo as a traitor to his religion. But he was convinced that he was a faithful interpreter of the Old Testament. He was proud of his ancestral traditions, and had no doubt that what he was doing was both worthwhile and necessary.

There was, however, one thing on which all the synagogues of the Roman world were united. This was in their use of the Greek language. As part of his ambitious plan to convert the whole world to Greek ways of thinking, Alexander the Great had imposed the Greek language and customs on those nations he conquered. In Palestine, this led to great resistance which ended in open revolt, though eventually Alexander's successors did manage to establish a degree of 'Hellenization' even there. But elsewhere, Jews were quite reconciled to the fact that they had to speak Greek. Indeed, as one generation succeeded another it was not long before the vast majority of Jews in the Mediterranean world could speak no other language, and so it became important that the ancient Jewish scriptures, originally written in Hebrew, should be translated into the language that most Jews now spoke and understood best.

The actual origins of the Greek Bible

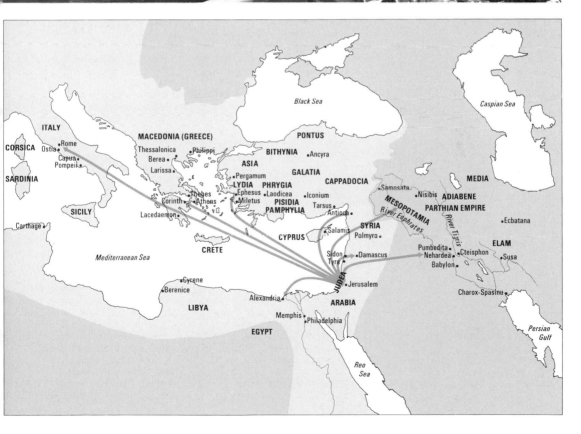

that was produced are shrouded in obscurity. According to one ancient legend, the Jews of Egypt managed to persuade the Egyptian king, Ptolemy II Philadelphus (285–247 BC) to sponsor the project. He sent to Jerusalem for seventy men who knew both Hebrew and Greek, and locked them up in seventy cells while each one produced his own translation. When their work was finished, to everyone's amazement the seventy men not only expressed the same ideas, but also used the very same Greek words to do so – whereupon Ptolemy was so impressed, that he was immediately convinced of the divine origins of their work! Not everyone believed that sort of story even in the ancient world, and another ancient source, 'The Letter of Aristeas', suggests that the translators set the precedent for all modern translations, and worked as a committee.

Probably neither of these stories by itself reflects what actually happened, and many scholars now believe that the Greek Septuagint version of the Old Testament (the LXX) just evolved gradually over many generations. But wherever it came from, it had enormous influence and importance. It was widely used not only by Jews all over the Roman Empire, but it was also read by intelligent Romans who wanted to know more about the Jewish faith – and it also became the Bible of the first Christian churches.

The majority of those who heard Peter's sermon on the Day of Pentecost were probably Greek-speaking Jews who had made a pilgrimage to Jerusalem for this great religious festival. Many of them would have been visiting Jerusalem for the first time. Though their homes were far away, they always had a warm regard for Jerusalem and its temple. This was the central shrine of their faith, just as it was for Jews who lived much nearer to it. Peter and the other disciples had no doubt that the good news about Jesus must also be shared with people like this. Indeed, they had much in common. The disciples themselves were regular supporters of the synagogue services. They too observed the great Jewish festivals, and on occasions they could even be found preaching within the temple precincts. This was something that Jesus himself had not been able to do without fear of the consequences, and though Peter and John were subsequently arrested and charged before the Jewish council, they were soon released, and the only restriction imposed on them was that 'on no condition were they to speak or to teach in the name of Jesus'. Apart from their curious belief in Jesus, their behaviour was generally quite acceptable to the Jewish authorities.

Acts 3:1-26

Acts 4:18

The conflict begins

Acts 6:1

Acts 6:2-6

But it was not long before all this was to change, for an argument arose between some Jews who spoke Greek (Hellenists) and others whose main language was Hebrew or Aramaic (Hebrews). They had all become Christians, perhaps on the Day of Pentecost, and some of these 'Hellenist' Christians were probably visitors to Jerusalem from other parts of the Roman Empire. But of course many Jews in Palestine also spoke Greek, and some of them may well have been permanent residents. At any event, those whose main language was Greek felt they were getting an unfair deal in the distribution of funds within the church. So alongside the twelve apostles who had the care of the more conservative Hebrew Christians, seven other men were appointed to supervise the arrangements for the Hellenistic Christians. Though most of them are just names to us, one of them – Stephen – soon demonstrated that he was at least as gifted in theological argument as he was in the administration of funds.

According to Acts, it all started as an argument within the 'synagogue of the Freedmen' in Jerusalem. It is not certain just who these 'Freedmen' were, but they were probably Jews who had come from other parts of the Roman Empire, released from some form of slavery, and had then formed their own synagogue in Jerusalem. Acts says that this synagogue congregation 'included Jews from Cyrene and Alexandria', and that they sided with others 'from the provinces of Cilicia and Asia' in debates with Stephen. Stephen himself was presumably a member of this synagogue, and no doubt he supposed that by sharing his new insights with other members of the synagogue he would be able to help them to the same belief in Jesus as he himself had reached. But it was not to be. Far from convincing his fellow Hellenists of the truth of the Christian claims,

The Western ('Wailing') Wall in Jerusalem is the only remaining part of the ancient temple and, as such, is a special place of prayer and devotion for Jews.

all he managed to do was to convince them that he was himself a heretic. And so they dragged him before the Jewish council, the Sanhedrin.

Acts 6:8-15

The story of Acts suggests that in order to bring effective charges, Stephen's accusers had to tell lies: 'This man', they said, 'is always talking against our sacred Temple and the Law of Moses. We heard him say that this Jesus of Nazareth will tear down the Temple and change all the customs which have come down to us from Moses!' There is a familiar ring about all this, for according to Mark this was one of the charges brought against Jesus at his trial. But whereas on that occasion the false witnesses failed to agree, and so other charges had to be found, in the case of Stephen he went on to condemn himself out of his own mouth.

Acts 6:13-14
Mark 14:57-59

Stephen's speech

The speech of Stephen before the Sanhedrin (Acts 7:1-53) is one of the longest speeches reported anywhere in the New Testament, and many people have found it difficult to see how it can be regarded as any sort of response to the charges that had been made against him. Because of this, some scholars have suggested that what we now have in Acts 7 was simply composed by the author of Acts as an appropriate theological explanation of why the Hellenist Christians began to move away from Jerusalem and to break their allegiance to Judaism. This question is not of course restricted to the story of Stephen: it is also relevant to the speeches allegedly delivered by Peter, Paul and others elsewhere in Acts. Were these speeches based on verbatim reports that were handed down to the author of Acts? Or did he follow the example of a writer like Josephus, who seems to have inserted speeches at will into the mouths of those whose exploits he describes? A number of points are relevant to this question:

● Obviously, none of the speeches reported in Acts can be verbatim accounts. They are far too short for that, and in any case people in the ancient world were not obsessed with the desire for accurate quotation which is so important to us today. We can see this quite clearly in the way some New Testament writers refer even to the Old Testament. Though it had supreme authority for them, they often do not quote it from any known version, but simply refer to it from memory – and often do so inaccurately as a result! In the case of Stephen's trial, it is unlikely that anyone would have taken down extensive notes of what was actually said. The impression one gets is that the whole thing took place with great urgency, quite unlike a major trial today.

The Greek historian Thucydides.

● At the same time, we also need to note that not all ancient historians were like Josephus. Josephus was a Jew. But the Greek tradition of history-writing is better represented by someone like Thucydides. He also felt that the inclusion of speeches at appropriate points in his narrative would help to highlight the important points. But he was not in the habit of simply inventing such speeches, as he explains in the beginning of his *History of the Peloponnesian War* (1.22.1): '. . . some speeches I heard myself, others I got from various quarters; it was in all cases difficult to carry them word for word in one's memory, so my habit has been to make the speakers say what was in my opinion demanded of them by the various occasions, of course adhering as closely as possible to the general sense of what they really said.'

● On more general grounds, Acts would appear to fit into the Thucydidean mould rather than following the traditions of a person like Josephus. Though its story of early Christianity is undoubtedly selective, when it can be tested against external evidence from the Roman Empire, it appears to be generally trustworthy.

● All the speeches in Acts at least have the appearance of authenticity. In subject matter, language and style they are varied to suit the people who make them. Certainly, so far as the Stephen speech is concerned, the content of the speech does fit in admirably with the kind of occasion that is described. Whenever dissidents of any kind are on trial for their lives, they often choose to defend not themselves, but the ideals for which they stand. And this is precisely what Stephen does. No doubt he had argued like this many times before within the synagogue itself, and no doubt others would repeat the arguments after him. To that extent, his speech is a confession of faith. It is not unrealistic to imagine that he would be determined to take his own last chance of standing before the highest Jewish authority and making sure his message was heard there too. It is certainly the sort of thing one can imagine having taken place – and in this respect it is quite different from the verbose and often irrelevant speeches which Josephus inserted into the mouths of many of his characters.

In his long speech before the Sanhedrin, Stephen not only admitted the truthfulness of the vague accusations made against him by the witnesses; he also went on to make very specific

Acts 7:1-53   statements about the subjects in dispute. With a carefully detailed survey of the history of Israel, he argued that the temple ought never to have existed at all. With copious quotations from and

Stephen brought down the full wrath of the Sanhedrin on his head by attacking the most precious and revered Jewish institution – the Jerusalem temple. He was taken outside the city wall and stoned.

1 Kings 5:4-5

allusions to the Old Testament, he pointed out how a simple tent of worship had been given to Moses by God as the place where he should be worshipped – and this had continued even long after the desert wanderings were over. It was only with the accession of Solomon to the throne of Israel that things started to change. With increased wealth and a new international political stature, Solomon had decided to build a central sanctuary in Jerusalem. The Old Testament suggests that he had divine approval for his actions, though strenuous religious and moral conditions were also imposed

1 Kings 9:1-9
Isaiah 66:1-2
to ensure the continued existence of the temple. But Stephen was quite sure that the temple had been a mistake from the start. Quoting the prophet Isaiah to support his argument, he asserted quite categorically that 'The Most High God does not live in houses Acts 7:48 built by men'. He then went on to accuse the Jewish leaders of wholesale disobedience to the very Law that they professed to Acts 7:53 uphold.

Not surprisingly, all this was too much for them. And when Stephen committed what they regarded as the final blasphemy by asserting that he could 'see heaven opened, and the Son of Man Acts 7:56 standing at the right hand side of God', he can hardly have been taken aback when he was dragged out of the council chamber and Acts 7:57-60 stoned to death.

Stephen's speech is almost unique in the New Testament. With the exception of Hebrews (see chapter three below), no other New Testament person or book has much to say about the temple and its services. But outside the New Testament, we have evidence of others who disapproved of what was going on there. At a much later date, the so-called *Epistle of Barnabas* adopts a very similar radical position on the Jewish temple – though there can be no question of Stephen having been familiar with that document, for it was not written until the early second century. Some of its strongly anti-Jewish sentiments could perhaps have been inspired by the story of Stephen in the New Testament.

But some scholars have suggested that Stephen's thinking could have been influenced by two religious groups in Palestine who did exist at the same time as him, and who also rejected the temple in Jerusalem. These were the people of Qumran, who wrote the Dead Sea Scrolls, and the Samaritans. Neither of them took part in worship at the temple, though their reasons for not doing so were rather different from the convictions that Stephen apparently held.

The Qumran community had imposed on themselves an enforced isolation from Jerusalem. Believing the temple and its priesthood to be corrupt, they had moved out to establish their own monastic commune by the shores of the Dead Sea. But they fervently believed that this state of affairs was only temporary. They were expecting the Messianic Age to come very soon, and then they themselves would be able to return to Jerusalem and restore the temple and its worship to its original purity. They did not despise the temple as an institution, as did Stephen. Instead, they deplored what they regarded as its temporary corruption.

The Samaritans were also unable to take part in the temple worship at Jerusalem, though for rather different reasons. It is not altogether clear just who the Samaritans of New Testament times actually were. It may be that they were descendants of people like Sanballat and Tobiah, who during and after the time of the Jewish exile in Babylon had collaborated with the foreign rulers of Nehemiah 6 Palestine. If so, pious Jews would naturally regard them as half-breeds and traitors – certainly unfit to worship in Jerusalem. On the other hand, it is quite likely that they had no connection at all with such people, and had arisen as a new Jewish sect of some kind in the years just before the beginning of the Christian era. In any event, they had their own sanctuary on Mt Gerizim and their own version of the Old Testament, which was substantially shorter than that used by the Jews themselves. The fact that they worshipped at Gerizim rather than Jerusalem formed the basis of the conversation between Jesus and a Samaritan woman, and it is interesting to see how that conversation ends on a note that was not altogether out of harmony either with Samaritan thinking or with the speech of Stephen: 'Jesus said, ". . . the time will come when people will not worship the Father either on this mountain or in Jerusalem . . . the time is coming and is already here, when by the power of God's Spirit people will worship the Father as he really is, offering him the true worship that he wants." '

John 4:19-24

John 4:21,23

There are obvious similarities between the thinking of the Qumran community and the Samaritans and Stephen, and the way that Stephen expounded the Old Testament is not unlike the way some of these other sects understood it. But it is highly unlikely that Stephen had ever been a member of either group. If he had been, it is hard to see how and why he could have been in Jerusalem in the first place.

It is more likely that his thinking on the temple, which was derived from the Old Testament, was brought out spontaneously as a result of the events of the Day of Pentecost and what followed. Through the presence and power of the Holy Spirit in the church, Christian believers now had direct access to God himself – and so the temple was redundant. It was at best an indirect means of worshipping God, and when men and women had direct access to him, then the temple became an unnecessary stumbling-block to those who were following Jesus.

Stephen's death

Did the Jewish Sanhedrin have the right to execute Stephen in the way they did? At the time, Judea was a Roman province, and in Roman provinces generally the right to execute even convicted criminals was reserved for the Roman governor and no one else. This point is brought out quite clearly in the stories of Jesus' trials and execution in the Gospels. According to John 18:31, the same Jewish leaders who were involved in Stephen's death had been forced to admit earlier to Pilate that 'we are not allowed to put anyone to death'.

This was not strictly accurate, for there was just one instance when the Sanhedrin was allowed to carry out a death sentence without reference to the Roman authorities. This was in the case of a person who violated the sanctity of the temple at Jerusalem. Anyone, even a Roman, who entered the temple unlawfully could be executed on the orders of the Sanhedrin (Josephus, *Jewish Wars* 6.2.4). But this was a special arrangement, which simply serves to emphasize the general powerlessness of the Sanhedrin. For if it already had general powers of jurisdiction in such cases, it would not have required this kind of special dispensation.

In view of the way that Stephen had spoken out against the temple, it is always possible that he may have been deemed to have violated the temple and its rights in some way. But it is more likely that his death was not the result of a formal sentence, so much as a mob lynching. Acts 7:54-60 does not suggest that any legal verdict was given, but rather that the Jewish leaders spontaneously stoned him in their fury. We do know of at least one other example of such behaviour, namely the execution of James of Jerusalem in AD 62.

The death of Stephen was undoubtedly one of the crucial events in the life of the early church, and its effects were soon to be felt not only in Jerusalem but throughout the rest of Palestine, and ultimately throughout the Roman Empire.

Persecution

One of its immediate consequences was a widespread persecution of the Christians in Jerusalem. Not many of them had adopted the same radical attitude towards the temple as Stephen. But it was inevitable that people should suppose that most, if not all Christians would think like him. And the Jews disliked it intensely, for Stephen was striking at the very roots of their most treasured beliefs. But persecution inevitably led to the dispersal of Christians from Jerusalem itself, especially those who were most sympathetic to the message of Stephen. Caesarea, Antioch and Damascus – not to mention other, more far-flung cities from which the Hellenist Christians had originally come – all witnessed a remarkable influx of these people. They were not just the first Christian refugees: they were also to be the first Christian missionaries. Though it was hardly what was intended, the Jewish persecutors of the church in Jerusalem were only encouraging it to spread to other parts of the land.

Acts 8:4

Not everyone had to leave Jerusalem. According to Acts, those who had shown themselves faithful to the principles of Judaism were able to stay, even in the face of such intense opposition. Luke mentions by name only the apostles, but it is certain that others must have stayed behind too – and all of them would be committed to some degree to Judaism as well as to their new faith in Jesus as the Messiah. This inevitably meant that the church in Jerusalem became more conservative and more rigidly Jewish, a fact that in due course led to its demise and the extinction of all Jewish forms of Christianity.

Acts 8:1

But Acts has very little to say about the church in Jerusalem at this time. Instead the attention shifts to the exploits of various Christian leaders elsewhere in Palestine.

Into Judea and Samaria

Philip is one of the Hellenist Christian leaders singled out for special mention in Acts, and he was no doubt typical of many others. We know comparatively little about him, but he was obviously very successful in communicating the Christian message to the inhabitants of other parts of Palestine, especially in Hellenistic cities like Caesarea. Some years later, he and his daughters were leading figures in a prosperous Christian community there. But before settling in Caesarea, he had a successful mission among the Samaritans too. We also have the story of how Philip met and baptized an African. This man was an Ethiopian bureaucrat, who was presumably an adherent of Judaism, since he was on his way home from visiting the temple in Jerusalem when Philip came across him in the desert. After an extended conversation about the meaning of the Old Testament, the man declared his faith in Jesus

Acts 21:8-9

Acts 8:4-25; 26-40

The church reaches out.

as the Messiah, and was baptized there and then.

Philip had little choice but to take his message outside Jerusalem. As one of the seven men appointed to oversee the funds for Hellenist Christians, he had been a close associate of Stephen, and it was no longer safe for him to stay in Jerusalem. But it was not long before some of the original disciples of Jesus also began to tour the countryside of Palestine with their message. We should not be surprised that men like Peter and John should have decided to leave Jerusalem. They were themselves countrymen, and Jerusalem was not their home. Moreover, though Jesus had no doubt visited Jerusalem on several occasions during his own lifetime, the main centre of his activity was not among the conventionally religious people there, but among the beggars and peasants of rural Palestine. So when Peter and John moved on to other areas, they were just following in their master's footsteps.

But they were clearly doing more than that. For the two of them together visited the Samaritans who had come to believe in Jesus as a result of Philip's preaching. It is easy to gain the impression from Acts that this was a kind of 'official inspection' of Philip's work – Peter and John giving the stamp of Jerusalem's approval to what he was doing. But a closer reading suggests that there was more to it than just that. For Peter and John were not afraid to identify themselves publicly with the work that Philip was doing. Not only did they accept his Samaritan converts as true Christians, but they also engaged in preaching among the Samaritans on their own initiative. And it was not long before Peter became involved in a travelling ministry over a wide area of the Palestinian countryside. Lydda, Joppa and even Caesarea itself were all on his itinerary.

Acts 8:14-17

Acts 8:25

Acts 9:32–10:48

Widening outreach

It was in the course of such travelling that Peter was to become convinced of the importance of non-Jewish people for the future of the Christian church. Of course, he himself had probably never been as conservative and traditionally Jewish as some of the church members whom he left behind in Jerusalem. The very fact that he was prepared to take his message to the more Hellenistic parts of Palestine is itself evidence of that. Then it is not insignificant that in the course of this tour, 'Peter stayed in Joppa for many days with a leather-worker named Simon'. No strictly orthodox Jew would have been prepared to do that, for workers in leather were generally regarded as being ritually unclean, since they were in constant contact with the skins of dead animals. But in this case, Peter was simply following the example of Jesus himself, who was not afraid to have close dealings with all kinds of outcasts of Jewish society.

While he was staying with this man, Peter had an experience that was to change his life. In a dream, he saw a large sheet full of 'all kinds of animals, reptiles and wild birds', many of them ritually unclean by the standards of the Old Testament food laws. So when a voice told him to help himself to some of these creatures, he naturally stated his unwillingness to do so – only to be rebuked by the voice, which he now recognized to be God's voice, telling him

Acts 9:43

Mishnah, Kelia 26.1-9

Luke 15:1-2

Acts 10:1-23

Acts 10:9-16

Mark 7:14-23

'Do not consider unclean anything that God has declared clean'. This was another lesson that Peter must have heard from the lips of Jesus himself. But in the tense atmosphere of Jerusalem after the death of Stephen, that can hardly have seemed an important principle, and Peter had adopted the more expedient course of following normal Jewish practices. But he was now to become caught up in something far larger than arguments about food, and what followed was to have far-reaching implications for the rest of his life's work.

No sooner had he woken from his dream than messengers arrived at the door of the house asking that he go to their master, Cornelius. This man was a Roman centurion in the main Roman garrison town, Caesarea, and Peter must have realized the serious implications of going there. But after his vision he had no choice, and so he entered Cornelius's house and accepted the Roman's

Acts 10:17-22

The message of Jesus was shown to be relevant for everyone, whether they lived in rural areas or sophisticated Hellenistic cities.

hospitality – something that was quite unthinkable to the Jewish Christians back in Jerusalem, whether on political or religious grounds. But as Peter spoke with these people, it became obvious that they were deeply interested in the Christian faith. As they listened, they responded to his message and Peter had to accept that they were true believers in Jesus, for they began to share in the same experience of the Holy Spirit as the first converts on the Day of Pentecost. At that, he was quite convinced that they should be baptized and accepted into the church; and as if to underline his own acceptance of them, Peter stayed in their home for a few days, no doubt instructing them further in their new faith.

Acts 10:24-48

This was a turning-point for Peter. When he got back to Jerusalem, his more conservative Jewish Christian friends were not at all pleased. Though his own account of the affair gave them some reassurance, it is obvious from the rest of Acts that this incident had

Acts 11:1-3

a deep and lasting effect on Peter's relationship with the church at Jerusalem. For it was not long before a man who had not been one of the original twelve disciples became the acknowledged leader of the church there: James, the brother of Jesus. In addition, it was not long after Peter's visit to Caesarea that Herod Agrippa I, the ruler of Palestine at the time, instituted an official persecution of the Christians in Jerusalem. As a result of this James, the brother of Acts 12:1-5 John, was martyred, and Peter himself put into prison. It may well

Joppa, modern-day Jaffa, was the scene of a radical about-turn in Peter's attitude to preaching the gospel to non-Jews.

have been that Peter's willingness to reach out to Gentiles with the Christian message gave Agrippa just the opportunity he was looking for to gain the sympathetic support of pious Jews for his actions against the church. If so, that would be an added reason why Peter soon fell from prominence among the Jewish Christians.

We know very little in detail about Peter's activities after this point. But what we do know connects him not with the Jewish churches of Palestine, but with the Hellenistic churches scattered throughout the Roman Empire. We know of an occasion when he Galatians 2:11-14 visited Antioch in Syria, and he also seems to have had some kind of 1 Corinthians 1–4 contact with the church in the Greek city of Corinth. He clearly travelled far and wide in the service of the gospel, often accompa-1 Corinthians 9:5 nied by his wife on his travels. And, according to well-attested traditions, he had strong connections with the church at Rome, and it was there that he was martyred for his faith in the persecution of Nero about AD 64.

To the ends of the earth

Acts 15:5

In the New Testament, the centre of interest moves away from Peter and the other disciples of Jesus to another important figure in the life of the early church – Paul, the Pharisee. He was not the only Pharisee to become a Christian, but he was certainly the best-known of them. Unlike many other Jewish Christians, Paul was not born in Palestine. Like many of the converts on the Day of Pentecost, he was a Hellenistic Jew. His home was in the city of Tarsus in the Roman province of Cilicia, and he was also a Roman citizen.

Acts 22:3, 27

Paul

As a Jewish child in Tarsus, Paul learned the traditions of his own people through regular instruction at the local synagogue. There he

Young Jewish boys learn the basics of the Hebrew alphabet at Yeshiva Religious School in Jerusalem. Paul received instruction in Jewish history and religious traditions at the synagogue in Tarsus and a rabbinical school in Jerusalem.

became familiar with the Greek Old Testament (the Septuagint), as well as learning about other aspects of his national heritage. But of course he also knew a great deal about Greek culture and ways of thinking, and Greek would have been his native language. He grew up in the same kind of environment as Stephen and the other Hellenist Jews who had caused such a stir in Jerusalem. In view of this, it may be more than a coincidence to find Paul taking an active interest in the trial and death of Stephen. He had come to Jerusalem some years earlier, to train in the school of the learned Rabbi Gamaliel. On his own account, he was a highly successful student: 'I was ahead of most fellow-Jews of my age in my practice of the Jewish religion, and was much more devoted to the traditions of our ancestors.'

Acts 7:58

Acts 22:3

Galatians 1:14

When Paul first appears in the pages of the book of Acts, he is nothing more than a coat-minder for those enraged Jews who stoned Stephen to death. But it was not long before Paul was to take

Acts 7:58; 8:1

Acts 8:3

a more active and personal part in persecuting Christians. As he saw the Hellenist Christians being forced out of Jerusalem he realized that, far from having stamped out this new religious sect, the persecution of Stephen and his friends was only helping the Christian cause to spread to other parts of the Roman Empire. There was little he could do to stop them going to Caesarea, for that was a city under Roman jurisdiction. Nor was Samaria a wise place for a Jewish rabbi to venture. But Damascus was different, for that was an independent city. It also had a large Jewish population who might be expected to co-operate with a rabbi from Jerusalem. Paul took advantage of the fact that at an earlier stage in his nation's history, the Romans had given the Jewish high priest the right to

1 Maccabees 15:15-24

have Jewish criminals extradited from other parts of the empire. So he went to the high priest to ask for a letter authorizing him to pursue the Christians to Damascus, and bring them back to

Acts 9:1-2

Jerusalem for trial and sentence. It was while doing so that Paul had a remarkable experience which was to alter the course of his whole life.

Paul's conversion

Acts 9:3; 26:13

As he was travelling with his entourage along the road to Damascus, 'a light from heaven, brighter than the sun' shone down on him, and he was challenged by a voice which he at once recognized as that of

Acts 9:4; 22:7; 26:14

the risen Christ, asking 'Why do you persecute me?' Paul's life was to take a radical about-turn. He immediately realized that the hopes he had previously entertained as a Jew were false. Jesus of Nazareth, whom, along with his followers, Paul had so despised, was standing before him as the Son of God and Lord of all, demanding that he should recognize Christ's rule over his nation, and over Paul's own life. And Paul responded by accepting these demands. The Pharisee who had hated the Christian faith was to become its greatest advocate. Though he might have boasted about his great achievements in Judaism, from now on his life was totally dominated by the risen Christ who appeared to him on the Damascus road, and revolutionized his life and thinking.

Yet Paul's remarkable conversion did not spring from nothing. No doubt he already knew a great deal about the life and teachings of Jesus of Nazareth. Indeed, some suggest that he may have been

2 Corinthians 5:16

personally acquainted with Jesus. But that is unlikely. What is certain, however, is that he must have taken a considerable interest in the kind of interpretation being placed on the Old Testament by Hellenist Jewish Christians like Stephen. Perhaps the very fact that he did not himself take part in the stoning of Stephen may suggest that he had an uncertain sympathy with what was being said. There can be little doubt that such thinking had an enormous and profound influence on his own life, for in many respects the teaching of Paul on the place of the Old Testament Law and covenants in the Christian life is but a logical extension of the teaching of those Hellenist Jews who were Christians before him. As a Christian, Paul was not much interested in the ritual and ceremonial aspects of the Old Testament Law. He was much more concerned about the Law as a source of morality – no doubt because of his own background as a Pharisee. But what he wrote about the temporary and passing nature of the Law in Galatians bears a striking similarity to Stephen's arguments about the Law and the temple in Acts.

Galatians 3:1-25

When he arrived in Damascus after his remarkable experience, Paul was still overwhelmed, and was unable to eat or drink for three days. But God had a plan for Paul's life that covered the details as well as the broad outline – and so Ananias, a Christian living in Damascus, came to visit Paul. He was able to restore Paul's sight, and at that Paul was baptized and spent some time with the Christians in Damascus. Like Peter in the household of Cornelius, Paul was now to discover that within the fellowship of the Christian church he could be united with men and women who on any other ground would have been abhorrent to him. But his experience was even more radical than that of Peter. For these people who had accepted him so generously were the very ones whom he had been intent on hounding to death. Instead of that, they now became his closest friends. It is hardly surprising that when he later wrote a letter to the churches of Galatia, the central burden of his message should be the conviction that men and women of different social and religious backgrounds could come together only through a living relationship with Jesus Christ: 'There is no difference between Jews and Gentiles, between slaves and free men, between men and women; you are all one in Christ Jesus.'

Acts 9:9

Acts 9:10-19; 22:12-16

Galatians 3:28

Paul the missionary

It was this burning conviction that inspired Paul to carry the Christian message not only to the cities of Palestine – places like Damascus itself, Antioch, and even Jerusalem – but also to the furthest corners of the known world. In doing so, he displayed an amazing vitality, and through the letters he wrote to many of his churches he has left us a priceless insight into what it must have been like to be a Christian in the wider Roman world of the first

The good news about Jesus Christ has been taken 'to the ends of the earth'. Here, Christians in Papua New Guinea celebrate the dedication of their first New Testament.

2 Corinthians 11:25-27

Galatians 2:20; Philippians 1:21

century AD. It was not all easy going, even for an apostle. Paul's long journeys must have been physically exhausting and highly dangerous. But Paul was undaunted. He was quite convinced that he was not alone in his endeavours. Indeed, they were not really *his* endeavours at all, for he was conscious of the living Christ of the Damascus road continuing to live within him throughout his life.

Paul travelled along the Egnatian Way, a busy Roman road, between Philippi and Thessalonica.

Philippians 3:8

From that moment onwards, his life was dominated by the desire to please his risen Lord, and everything else was trivial by comparison. Writing towards the end of his life, he put it like this: 'I count everything as loss because of the surpassing worth of knowing Christ Jesus my Lord.'

Paul and the earliest church

The story of Paul's life and letters is examined in greater detail in *Paul*, a companion book to this one. But we cannot leave him here without first asking a number of important questions about his work and its relationship to the other apostles. When we read the New Testament, it is not difficult to get the impression that only two people really mattered in the early church: Jesus himself, and Paul. For the stories of Jesus in the Gospels and the writings of Paul together account for something like three-quarters of the whole New Testament. We occasionally meet Peter, James and other lesser characters such as Silas or Timothy on the pages of Paul's letters. But even in Acts, they seem to take a back seat to Paul himself. Of course, there are reasons for this, no doubt connected with the purpose for which Acts was written in the first place. It is on any account a selective story of the beginnings of Christianity. For example, if we only had Acts to go by, we might suppose that Paul was the first Christian to take the gospel to Rome. But we know from his letter to the church in that city that a large and thriving Christian fellowship existed there long before he visited Italy. So Paul's work, though of fundamental importance, was clearly complementary to that of many other figures in the early church, whose names and exploits have not been recorded for us.

Romans 1:6-7

But was Paul's work really complementary to that of Peter and other early Christian leaders – or was he instead establishing a different brand of Christianity altogether, different from the original church at Jerusalem not only in character, but in belief as well?

That was the suggestion put forward in the middle of the nineteenth century by the members of the so-called 'Tübingen School' in Germany. Influenced by the great New Testament scholar, Ferdinand Christian Baur, they argued that there was a vast difference between Paul's type of Christianity and the sort of churches founded by Jewish Christians such as Peter, or James of Jerusalem. They saw the whole of the first generation of Christianity as a conflict between these rival forms of Christian belief – a conflict that was resolved only with the emergence of the catholic church in the second century. This was not a new idea. Even in the second century, the anonymous authors of the *Clementine Homilies* and *Recognitions* were suggesting that there were irreconcilable differences between Paul and the original apostles.

But is this a fair picture, either of Paul or of the others? Was he really independent of the Jewish base of the church in Jerusalem? Or do we today just like to think that he was, perhaps because his more open-minded view of the gospel is, in general, more acceptable to our own modern outlook?

When we examine the New Testament closely, whether in Paul's own writings or in the stories of Acts, it soon becomes clear that Paul was much more conscious of his own Jewish origins and background than many modern scholars are prepared to allow. At a number of points he goes out of his way to establish some sort of continuity between his own Gentile churches on the one hand, and the earliest Jewish church, and even Judaism itself, on the other.

Christians and the Old Testament

It is significant that when Paul defines Christian faith, he consistently does so in relation to Judaism. Take his letter to the Galatians, for example, the argument of which is also closely followed in Romans. The Galatian churches were being infiltrated by people claiming that in order to be a Christian one also needed to be a Jew (either by being born one or by accepting circumcision and the Old Testament Law). Paul found that quite abhorrent for, he claimed, a living relationship to God through Jesus Christ depended on simple trust ('faith'). And, he argued, it had always been so. Long before the Old Testament Law had even come into existence, Israel's ancestor Abraham had trusted God's promises, and had found fellowship with God on that basis. Therefore, anyone who wanted to be a part of God's covenant people needed only to follow the example of Abraham, and trust God. The Law was in some ways an aberration from the original simplicity of the relationship between Abraham and God.

Galatians 2:15

Galatians 3:6-9

To us today, the argument of Galatians can be somewhat difficult to read and understand. But it is occasionally obscure to us precisely because of its Jewish nature. Though Paul disagreed with the argument that in order to please God a person needed to accept the Jewish Law and customs, nevertheless he accepted without question the more basic premise that in order to please God a person must become a part of the covenant nation which had its historical origins in the Old Testament stories of the call of Abraham. In a sense, he was agreeing with those Jewish Christians who said that Gentiles must become Jews in order to be Christians. But, while they supposed that obedience to the Law was the hallmark of the real Jew, Paul redefined 'Jewishness' to lay all the emphasis instead on continuity with Abraham. To be a child of God was to be a member of Abraham's family – and to join that, faith in God was the only required qualification.

Galatians 3:6-25; 4:21-31

This Jewish boy has portions of the Law in tiny leather 'phylacteries', in literal obedience to the instruction in Deuteronomy 6:8 to tie the commands of the Lord 'on your arms and wear them on your foreheads'.

Paul continued this line of argument in his letter to the church at Rome. Indeed, there he added the comment that 'the real Jew is the person who is a Jew on the inside . . . and this is the work of God's Spirit, not of the written Law'. In saying this, he stands in the same tradition as Stephen, and the Old Testament prophets before him. Racial pedigree was not the most important thing, but obedience to God's will. But we should notice here that, no matter how he redefined the Old Testament faith in relation to the Judaism of his own day, Paul always felt it important that Christians, whether Jews or Gentiles, should be seen within the context of the continuing actions of God in history that had begun with Abraham, and would receive their final fulfilment and consummation at some future time. Unlike some of his later admirers, Paul never suggested that the Old Testament was irrelevant for the Christian. Instead, he saw even Gentile Christians as part of a great line of faith stemming from Abraham himself, and this qualified them to be a part of 'the Israel of God'. This line of argument has close similarities to the thinking of Peter, as we shall see in chapter three below.

Romans 2:29

Galatians 3:29

Galatians 6:16

The church and Israel

The most difficult passage in the whole of Paul's writings makes all this even more explicit. This is what he writes in Romans chapters 9–11. Scholars are undecided as to how this section of Romans fits into its context. Some argue that this is the key that unlocks the door to the whole of the rest of the letter. Others believe it was an afterthought, representing Paul's uncertain speculations on the fate of the Jewish people, rather than any kind of carefully developed thinking on the subject. Whichever view we take, there can be no

Paul uses the imagery of an olive tree to describe the Jewish nation, onto which Gentile Christians have been 'grafted'.

The countryside of Cilicia,
modern-day southern Turkey, was
familiar ground to Paul on his
missionary journeys.

doubt about what Paul actually says here. For whatever reason, he quite clearly asserts that to be born a Jew still carries a distinct advantage. He compares the whole 'people of God' (the Israelites of the Old Testament, together with the Gentile Christians) to an olive tree. The roots of this tree go down deep into the Old Testament, and Gentile Christians have been grafted like a new branch onto this plant. In the meantime, some of the original (Jewish) branches have been broken off. But they will in due course be restored, says Paul. Indeed, the present situation is a temporary one. Though it may seem to some that 'the people of God' are now the Gentile Christians, God has allowed them to come in only to encourage the Jewish people to further obedience: 'Because they sinned, salvation has come to the Gentiles, to make the Jews jealous of them . . . but the stubbornness of the people of Israel is not permanent, but will last only until the complete number of Gentiles cries to God. And this is how all Israel will be saved.'

Romans 11:13-24

Romans 11:11, 25-26

On that rather cryptic note, Paul leaves his discussion of the subject. There are many difficulties in understanding precisely what he meant. But however he thought this was to be accomplished, Paul clearly believed that the Jews had an important part to play in the whole history of salvation – and this in itself suggests that he was by no means as implacably anti-Jewish as some have suggested.

To the Jews first

Acts 13:14; 14:1; 17:1-2

When we examine his practice, we find the same emphasis. Whenever he went to a new town in some hitherto unvisited part of the Roman world, Paul always went first to the Jewish synagogue. Of course, there would be good tactical reasons for doing so. Since he was concerned to declare that Jesus was the Messiah, it was only natural that he should speak first to people who had some notion of who and what the Messiah might be. The fact that they had rather different expectations from Paul himself usually became clear fairly quickly, as he was thrown out of one synagogue after another. But that did not stop him following the practice. Indeed, he makes it clear in Romans that, in addition to the practical advantages, he also had a strong theological reason for working like this: '. . . the gospel . . . is God's power to save all who believe, first the Jews and also the Gentiles.'

Romans 1:16

Jews and Gentiles

Galatians 2:7-9

Despite this, Paul believed he was specifically called to take the good news about Jesus to Gentiles rather than Jews. According to his letter to the Galatians, this special commission was recognized by the Jewish church leaders in Jerusalem: Paul would go to Gentiles, they to Jews. Inevitably, this was not a hard and fast rule. Paul often met and spoke with Jews, while Peter in particular was to become involved in missionary activity among Gentiles. But as a rough arrangement, it was a satisfactory division of labour. It may well have been agreed for social and economic reasons rather than for purely theological ones. Paul, as an unmarried person, was singularly well fitted to long and arduous journeys in a way that the

Palestinian apostles were not. They had wives and families, and needed to depend for their support on the regular generosity of the churches, whereas Paul could move about the empire quite freely, finding casual work to support himself as the need arose.

Acts 18:3; 2 Thessalonians 3:8

There are many complex problems involved in understanding the accounts of Paul's dealings with the leaders of the Jerusalem church, and more extensive consideration of them is to be found in *Paul*, pages 36-55. But the fact remains that Paul evidently had regular and not unfriendly contacts with the leaders of the church there.

Paul and Jerusalem

But was it more than that? Was Paul, as some have argued, almost under the control of the Jerusalem leaders? Do his letters conceal the truth in some way, making him appear much more independent than he actually was? This suggestion has gained some support from the fact that towards the end of his third missionary tour, Paul put a great deal of effort and energy into taking a collection among the Gentile Christians of Greece and Asia Minor, which was to be for the benefit of the church in Judea. We know from other sources that Hellenistic Jews throughout the empire sent an annual temple tax to the authorities in Jerusalem, to support the temple and its services there. So could the Jerusalem church exercise some kind of central control on the whole Christian movement by imposing a similar burden on the churches of Gentile believers founded by Paul?

1 Corinthians 16:1-7

It seems unlikely. In Romans, Paul outlines his own understanding of the collection: '. . . the churches in Macedonia and Achaia have freely decided to give an offering to help the poor among God's people in Jerusalem. That decision was their own . . .' He goes on to add, however, that 'as a matter of fact, they have an obligation to help them. Since the Jews shared their spiritual blessings with the Gentiles, the Gentiles ought to use their material blessings to help the Jews'. In other words, conscious of his own deep indebtedness to the Jewish Christian church, Paul had organized this collection as a kind of thank-offering and spontaneous expression of love for the Christians in Jerusalem. Of course, the Jewish Christians may well have seen it in a different light. It has been suggested that they would think of it as the fulfilment of the ancient prophecies of Isaiah, which speak of 'the wealth of the nations' being brought to Jerusalem, and its Gentile bearers 'bowing down to show their respect'.

Romans 15:26-27

2 Corinthians 8:8-14

Isaiah 60

If that were the case, however, we might expect them to have received Paul and his Gentile Christian companions with open arms. But in fact it is not clear what happened to the collection when it finally arrived in Jerusalem. It has been suggested that the Jewish Christians actually refused to accept it. And it is certainly striking that when Paul was subsequently arrested in the temple at Jerusalem, his fellow Jewish Christians did not spring to his defence. That was left to a Roman. Perhaps the Jewish Christians had not gone so far as to lead him into some sort of trap, but at least

Acts 21:27-40

they were not sorry to see the last of him. The same cannot however, be said of Paul's attitude to them. The very fact that he had made the effort to return to Jerusalem at this time shows his deep and lasting indebtedness to the leaders of the first Christian church.

Paul and the teaching of Jesus

This indebtedness also comes out in the way Paul often displays knowledge of and familiarity with the teachings of Jesus himself One of the most intriguing features of Paul's letters is the complete absence from them of any direct references to the life and teaching of Jesus. At one time it was fashionable to suggest that Paul had no time for Jesus, and that his own brand of Christianity was based instead on Greek and Roman concepts. But this kind of argument does not square with the facts.

While Paul very rarely makes a direct reference to Jesus teaching, there are several sections of his writings which bear a remarkable similarity to what we find in the Gospels. Occasionally Paul does say that he is quoting from or referring to 'words of the Lord'. But there are many other places where his own advice is so close to the teaching of Jesus as we know it from the Gospels that Paul must have been referring to it – for example, in the practical advice given to the church in Rome.

1 Corinthians 7:10; 9:14; 1 Thessalonians 4:15

● Love your enemies	Matthew 5:43-48
	Romans 12:14-21
● Love God and your neighbour	Mark 12:29-31
	Romans 13:8-10
● Teaching on 'clean' and 'unclean' foods	Mark 7:14-23
	Romans 14:14
● Responsibility to state authorities	Mark 12:13-17
	Romans 13:1-7

Galatians 1:18

Paul's knowledge of the words and deeds of Jesus had not come from personal contact with Jesus, but from those who had been Jesus' first disciples – especially, perhaps, from Peter with whom Paul spent two full weeks after his conversion. Paul must have known a great deal more about Jesus' teaching than we would guess from his letters. But there are reasons for his apparent silence on the matter. For one thing, his letters are occasional writings rather than considered and carefully worked out accounts of his whole theology. And then, it is also likely that his readers already knew a lot about the life and teaching of Jesus. Paul must have told them about this when he first told them the good news of the Christian message. He could not have spoken meaningfully about Jesus either to Gentiles or to Hellenist Jews without at the same time giving them some explanation about who Jesus was! And to be able to do that, he needed the co-operation and friendship of the original Jewish disciples.

Taken together, these six points suggest that, far from being an odd man out, Paul was part and parcel of the Christian movement as it began among the first Jewish disciples of Jesus. Of course he did not see eye to eye with the legalistic viewpoint of Jewish Christian leaders such as James. But he does not seem to have been out of line with the missionary outlook of someone like Peter. We have less knowledge of Peter's activities than we have about Paul's, but what we do know shows that he was engaged in missionary work of a very similar kind. Peter was no more at home than Paul in the church at Jerusalem, and as things turned out the Jerusalem church eventually found itself in a dead end. With the destruction of the city itself by the Roman armies in AD 70, the Christian witness there more or less disappeared for all practical purposes. The church's future lay not in the eastern extremities of the Roman Empire, but in the great towns and cities of the west – not least in Rome itself.

The dramatic events of AD 70, when the Roman armies destroyed Jerusalem and plundered the Temple, are depicted on the Titus Arch in Rome.

Paul and the non-Jewish world

There were many problems of a different kind to be overcome between Jerusalem and Rome. Though the Jewish religion was very popular even among well-educated Gentiles in the Roman Empire it was by no means the only religious system with which Paul had to wrestle.

For centuries before the coming of Jesus, the Greeks and Romans had worshipped their own gods and goddesses. Their actual relevance to the lives of ordinary people had often been called into question. They were worshipped in great festivals and complex rituals, but they existed in a world of their own. And when their devotees were in need, there was no guarantee that the gods and goddesses would do anything to help them. Indeed, by the time of the New Testament the speculations of Greek philosophers had placed serious question-marks against these old gods. Could intelligent people really believe in their existence any more? Were the stories of their doings not inherently unbelievable?

Many people were happy to adopt the rationalist scepticism of philosophers like Plato – or the Stoics and Epicureans who in the New Testament period had elevated 'Reason' to the most important principle in the universe. But not many people were attracted by philosophy itself, and the average person in the street was afflicted by what has been called 'a failure of nerve'. The certainties of the old religions had been swept away by the philosophers. But these themselves were so difficult to understand that for most people

Acts 14:8-13

Acts 17:16-34

Opposite, above: As well as worshipping the major gods and goddesses, the Romans also made regular offerings to the *Lares*, the household gods of good fortune. Little bronze figures stood in a special shrine just inside the front door of the house.

Opposite, below: From the Etruscans the Romans learned the art of divination by the examination of the intestines of animal sacrifices, and such practices continued until the end of the empire in the fifth century AD.

Below: Christians in the early church had to confront the power of Hellenistic culture and thought. This fragment from a second-century Christian sarcophagus shows a philosophical discussion in progress.

philosophy was not a realistic alternative. And so there was a religious vacuum.

Inevitably, there was no shortage of religions trying to fill the gap. Strange cults were trying to combine ideas from Eastern religions such as Zoroastrianism with ideas from the religious traditions of Egypt, Greece and Rome. These were the 'mystery religions', and large numbers of people were attracted to them. They claimed to offer an emotional satisfaction to those who had discarded the gods of ancient Greece and Rome as mere superstitions, but who found philosophy dull and beyond their mental grasp. These mystery religions offered a personal 'salvation' by means of secret rituals and complex initiations, and were often serious rivals to the Christian faith.

Paul had dealings with all these aspects of religion in the Roman Empire. When he and Barnabas restored the health of a lame man in the city of Lystra, the crowds in the market-place concluded that they must be the old Greek gods come down in person. The priest of the temple of Zeus, the chief Greek god, prepared to offer sacrifices to them – and Paul and Barnabas had great difficulty persuading him not to do so. Not long after this, at Athens, Paul was involved in debates with the Epicureans and Stoics – Greek philosophers – who seem to have had considerable difficulty in grasping his message. And it was only a short time later that he became involved in a complex and lengthy correspondence with the church

at Corinth. Much of the trouble there seems to have stemmed from the fact that some Christians were trying to import the beliefs and practices of the mystery religions into the church itself. This was a problem that was to become increasingly difficult for the church to solve. We can see traces of it throughout the New Testament, and it continued well into the second century.

The one thing that pagans in the Roman Empire could not understand about the Christians was their unwillingness to combine their beliefs about Jesus with other ideas that were floating around in the religious atmosphere of the Hellenistic world. To many people, one religion was as good, or as bad, as any other. They were quite happy to combine elements from different religions to suit their own outlook and temperament. But for Paul this was unacceptable. If Jesus was 'Lord', then neither Zeus nor Jupiter, nor any of the mystery gods and goddesses – still less the Roman emperor – could also be 'Lord'. To be a Christian was something distinctive and different, and Jesus himself must be the sole authority: 'For God has already placed Jesus Christ as the one and only foundation, and no other foundation can be laid.'

1 Corinthians 3:11

Paul was no more willing to dilute the Christian message with pagan elements than he was to accept Jewish beliefs about the Law and circumcision. His own life had been totally revolutionized by just one person – Jesus – and he was quite sure that all men and women could find true fulfilment in life only through a living relationship with him. Not only was Jesus the final expression of God's character. He was also someone who could be known as a personal friend. Moreover, his living presence was a source of great power, enabling the Christian to do what was right. So why should Jesus be confused with Greek and Roman gods, or mystery gods – or the god of Reason created by the philosophers? Paul had found all his needs – intellectual, emotional and moral – met in Jesus and he was convinced that others too would find the answer to life's problems only by whole-hearted obedience to him, whether they lived in Jerusalem, or Rome, or any other point between the two.

Colossians 1:15-20

Galatians 2:19-20; 5:16-26

The church in Galilee

Apart from occasional visits to Jerusalem, Jesus spent most of his life in Galilee. The majority of his followers must have lived there – many thousands of them, according to the Gospels. Yet Galilee is hardly ever mentioned in the story of early Christianity. Instead, the New Testament lays all the emphasis on the followers of Jesus in Jerusalem and in the Gentile cities of the Roman Empire.

It is not difficult to see the reasons for this. Luke is the only New Testament writer to produce anything like a history of the church, and he himself was probably a Gentile. His own main interest was therefore in the work of

Paul and others who took the gospel to people like himself. For Luke and his readers, Palestine was a remote outpost of the empire, and small internal distinctions, like the difference between Galilee and Judea, were insignificant to people who scarcely knew the location of either of them. In his Gospel, we can see how Luke does not always distinguish the two quite as carefully as the other Gospel writers, and in his history of early Christianity the only real division he makes is that between Jewish Christians and Gentile Christians. But a native of Palestine would not have seen it like that. The Judeans had no time for the people of Galilee. It was too open to

Gentile influences for their liking, and the fact that Jesus originated there was to many people a good reason for paying no attention to him (John 1:46).

But in spite of the fact that followers of Jesus in Galilee would tend to be ignored by Gentile Christians and despised by those from Jerusalem, they must nevertheless have continued to flourish. Great movements like that built up by Jesus do not vanish overnight, especially in a rural area. So what happened to his followers in Galilee? Some have suggested that they simply faded away. Some of them had no doubt gone to Jerusalem with Jesus, expecting him to set up a new nationalist government to overthrow the Roman rule, and when he died in apparent defeat they went back home to look for another leader. There must have been some who thought like that: Judas Iscariot may have been one of them. But not all Jesus' followers went with him on his last journey to Jerusalem, and not all of them had an exclusively political view of his message. No doubt these others would continue the work that Jesus had started in Galilee, perhaps developing their own churches in complete independence of what was going on in Jerusalem. A number of facts seem to support such a view:

● Galilee had always been quite

different from Jerusalem. It had its own ways of doing things, and its own religious traditions, most of which were despised by the more orthodox and conservative Jews in Jerusalem. It is unlikely therefore that the church in Jerusalem would have wanted any involvement in affairs in Galilee, and still less probable that the Galilean followers of Jesus would have been prepared to accept the authority of the Jerusalem church and its leaders.

● The very character of these leaders must have been an influential factor in the development of the Galilean church. After the expulsion of the Hellenists, the church in Jerusalem seems to have adopted a very conservative Jewish outlook. The priests and Pharisees whom Jesus had strongly opposed soon rose to positions of authority even in the church (Acts 6:7; 15:5), and it is quite likely that James, the main Jerusalem leader, was himself a Pharisee. They were now Christians, of course, and accepted Jesus as their Messiah. But that seems to have made little difference to their outlook and behaviour. They still held that the Jewish Law and customs were of special importance, as we can see from their attitude to Peter after he had stayed with Cornelius (Acts 11:1-4). It was no coincidence that Peter and the other original disciples did not

Jesus did not fulfil the expectations of some of his followers who were looking for a nationalist leader preaching a political solution to the country's problems.

stay long in Jerusalem. Persecution from the authorities and opposition from the Jerusalem church soon forced them to leave the city – and most of them must have gone back home, to Galilee.

● This also fits in with what we know about Peter, and enables us to guess at what he was doing between the time when he left Jerusalem and the time when we find him travelling the Roman Empire with the message of Jesus. Perhaps it was in Galilee that he was able to give more time and thought to this whole question of non-Jewish followers of Jesus. According to early church traditions, the Gospel of Mark contains the kind of things that Peter used to tell people about Jesus, and it is interesting to note how Mark's Gospel always shows the people of Galilee responding to the Christian message, while Jerusalem rejects it. Perhaps this reflects Peter's thinking about the development of the church at Jerusalem during this period.

● Two other New Testament books have also been connected with the Galilean churches: James and Hebrews Both of them have clear Jewish connections, but are difficult to identify with the kind of beliefs that were held in the church at Jerusalem. James has a very simple view of the Christian message – very similar to the message of Jesus himself as we know it from the Gospels, while Hebrews also has many references to the teachings of Jesus. It also sets out to show that Jerusalem and its temple are irrelevant – something that would be welcomed by Galileans. Both these books are discussed in more detail in chapter three.

We can never be sure exactly what happened to the followers of Jesus in Galilee, for no one wrote down their story. But there is enough evidence to suggest that the movement started there by Jesus did not die out, but probably grew and flourished at least for the lifetime of his original disciples.

The Acts of the Apostles

Every book of the New Testament tells us something about the history of the early church. The letters written by Paul and other Christian leaders are the kind of information which modern social historians would use and value, while even the Gospels tell us a great deal about their first readers. But the book of Acts tries to set out the early history of Christianity in some kind of orderly way. It is the sequel to the Gospel of Luke, and the two books belong together. They were both written to the same person, 'Theophilus', the Gospel to tell the story of the life and teaching of Jesus, and the book of Acts to tell how the work of this one person had developed into a worldwide Christian movement.

Acts does not in fact tell the story of all the apostles. Only some of them are mentioned extensively, and the book has most to say about Peter and Paul, together with a few incidents from the lives of other early Christian leaders such as Philip, John, James the brother of Jesus, and Stephen. The story is told in two parts. The first is concerned mainly with events in Jerusalem and elsewhere in Palestine, and here Peter is the leading character (chapters 1–12). The second section of the book tells the remarkable story of Paul (chapters 13–28). The two stories are not entirely unconnected. Paul makes his first appearance at the stoning of Stephen (Acts 7:58), while Peter is still involved at the time of the so-called Council of

Jerusalem, which is essentially a part of the story of Paul (Acts 15:7-11).

The author

Who wrote the book of Acts? Or, to put the question more accurately, who wrote the two volumes, Luke and Acts? There is no doubt they were both written by the same person. They are both addressed to Theophilus, and their style and language are identical. All the evidence points to Luke, the Gentile doctor who accompanied Paul on some of his travels.

The date

The date of Acts is a more controversial issue, and three main suggestions have been put forward:

The Second Century. The Tübingen School of F. C. Baur believed that Acts must have been written sometime after AD 100, and this view has been revived in recent years by the American scholar, Professor John Knox. Two main arguments are put forward to support this:

● Acts 5:36-37 refers to two individuals called Theudas and Judas, and 21:38 mentions an Egyptian troublemaker. Since Josephus' *Antiquities of the Jews* 20.5.1 seems to describe the same events, and since this was not published until AD 93, Acts, it is claimed, must have been written later than that. But there is no evidence to support the idea that Luke had actually read Josephus' stories. In fact, his description of these people is different from what Josephus says, and it is only possible to connect the two by supposing that Luke misunderstood Josephus' story when he read it.

● It is also suggested that Acts was written in about the middle of the second century to counteract the influence of the heretic Marcion. Among other things, Marcion was suggesting that the first disciples of Jesus had misunderstood the point of his teaching, and that Paul was the only true interpreter of Jesus. It is certainly true that Acts was read with renewed interest at the time of Marcion, for its story shows little sign of the kind of misunderstanding that Marcion emphasized. But there is no real trace of second-century concerns in the book – while there is plenty of evidence to connect it with the period that it purports to describe.

AD 62–70. At the opposite extreme, other scholars suggest that Acts was written almost at the same time as the events it describes – either immediately after the arrival of Paul in Rome (62–64, according to F. F. Bruce and J. A. T. Robinson), or shortly after his death (66–70, in the view of T. W. Manson and, hesitatingly, C. S. C. Williams). The following arguments are said to favour such an early date:

● By any standards, Acts ends very abruptly. Paul arrives in Rome, and the last we see of him he is 'teaching about the Lord Jesus Christ quite openly and unhindered' (Acts 28:31). It must be said, however, that this is the natural climax of Luke's story. He said at the outset that he would relate the progress of the gospel from Jerusalem to Rome (Acts 1:8), so perhaps nothing further needed to be said. But the modern reader is inevitably curious to know whether Paul appeared before the emperor's court, and if so what happened to him. We are not the first ones to ask these questions, and there are ancient traditions claiming to give us the answers. Eusebius, one of the early church historians, says that 'after defending himself the apostle was sent again on his ministry of preaching, and coming a second time to the same city, suffered martyrdom under Nero' (*Ecclesiastical History* 2.22). A statement in 1 Clement 5 (written about AD 95) suggests that Paul visited Spain during this short time of freedom, while some modern scholars would like us to think that it was during this time that Paul penned the so-called Pastoral Epistles (1 and 2 Timothy and Titus). We do not

really know whether Paul went on such further travels. But there is no reason to doubt that he ultimately died as a martyr in Rome during the persecution ordered by Nero in AD 64.

Because of this, it is suggested that if Acts was written after Paul was dead, then the statement about him preaching openly and unhindered is an odd note on which to finish the story of his life. But this kind of argument is double-edged. Since Paul is Luke's hero, surely it would be at least as likely that he would present his life ending in the triumph of his preaching in Rome as that he would finish his story with the apparent defeat of martyrdom. It is always haphazard to try and guess what this or that ancient writer may or may not have written in given circumstances. We can really only guess at what we might have written ourselves had we been there – and even then we cannot be sure, since at this distance from the events we do not know all the facts. So this argument in favour of an early date for Acts really carries very little objective weight.

● A more substantial argument is that the book of Acts has a generally favourable attitude to the Roman authorities. Paul's Roman citizenship is an asset to him, giving him freedom to travel in peace all over the empire. When he meets Roman officials, they are always on his side: Sergius Paulus, the proconsul of Cyprus who became a Christian (Acts 13:6-12); Gallio, the proconsul in Corinth who gave him a fair hearing (Acts 18:12-17); even the Roman commander in Jerusalem who rescued him from a hostile Jewish mob (Acts 21:31-40). They all look favourably on Paul's mission, and the impression is given that, if the empire is not exactly supporting the church, it certainly is not at enmity with it. But of course all that changed in AD 64, with the great persecution instituted by Nero, and official persecution of one sort or another was to continue spasmodically right through to the end of the first century. So again it is argued that Acts must have been written prior to AD 64. But again this is a subjective judgement, for it implies that the events of the author's own day would colour his historical judgement. But if Acts can be regarded as a reasonably faithful presentation of the period it describes, then its apparent pro-Roman bias may simply reflect the facts of the situation.

● Acts does not seem to give any hint of the Fall of Jerusalem, which took place in AD 70, and if Jerusalem had been destroyed before Acts was written, it is claimed that we would have

Nero ruled from AD 54 to 68 and was the first Roman emperor to persecute the Christians.

expected a mention of the fact. For it would have been a striking vindication of Luke's viewpoint on Judaism and indeed on Jewish Christianity. Again, this argument depends on the assumption that we can know precisely what was in the mind of an ancient author, and what he might be expected to write in given circumstances.

● Another relevant fact is that Acts makes no mention at all of the letters that Paul wrote to his churches. So far as the date of Acts is concerned, this undoubtedly suggests that it was written before the letters were collected together and circulated, and so Acts must be earlier than a writing like 2 Peter, which mentions Paul's letters as a part of sacred Scripture (2 Peter 3:16).

AD 80–85. Many scholars feel that there is no justification for either a very late second-century date for Acts, or a very early date in the sixties of the first century. Instead, they prefer to date it sometime in the eighties of the first century. Two substantial reasons have been put forward for this:

● Acts begins with the words: 'In my first book I wrote about all the things which Jesus did and taught' (Acts 1:1). This 'first book' was Luke's Gospel. But we know that when he wrote this, Luke incorporated stories and sayings of Jesus that he took from the Gospel that had already been written by Mark. And since Mark seems to have written his Gospel sometime between 60 and 65, this means that we can hardly date Luke's first volume much earlier than about 65–70. This in turn means that Acts, as the second volume, cannot have been written as early as 62–64.

This is a persuasive argument, though it is not absolutely convincing. It has at least two weak spots. First, it depends on the date we give to Mark. But we have no absolutely certain indications of when that Gospel was written. The general consensus may be right. On the other hand, it may not, and when John Robinson, for instance, urges a much earlier date for Mark, he does have some evidence in his favour. Second, it is also possible that the prologues of both Luke and Acts were added last, when the two books were in their final form. Many competent scholars believe that Luke's Gospel originally existed in a shorter version before Luke came across Mark's work ('Proto-Luke'), and Acts could also have been written in stages. The passages where Luke uses 'we' rather than 'they' may have been just the first of several editions of Luke's story of the early church. This original account may later have been expanded to include stories about the early

Jerusalem church, perhaps brought to Luke's attention during his stay in Caesarea while Paul was in prison there. So it is always possible that the basic core of Acts could have been written before the Gospel, with only the prologue being added later to commend it to Theophilus.

● But there is a more substantial reason for dating Acts later than the lifetime of Paul. Luke's writing often seems to show signs of attitudes and beliefs which were common in the post-apostolic age. Indeed, Luke and Acts together are sometimes regarded as a kind of manifesto of what scholars refer to as 'early catholicism'. This subject is dealt with in some detail in the next chapter. It is argued there that the emergence of so-called 'catholic Christianity' was a natural, almost imperceptible development of certain elements within the teaching of the apostles themselves. Here we should simply note that Luke does have a distinctive outlook, and that in some respects this outlook corresponds to the development of early catholic thinking.

For instance, reading only Acts one might well get the impression that the early church had a largely uncontroversial existence. But as we read Paul's letters, it becomes obvious that there is another side to the picture. No doubt it was a part of Luke's intention to stress that there was fundamental agreement between all sections of the early church. And, up to a point, Paul himself accepted this, for he goes out of his way to emphasize his own continuity with the earliest disciples. But it is only part of the picture. For Paul's letters also show that he often had profound disagreements not only with his enemies, but with his friends as well. Paul often emerges from his letters as a very impulsive person, and it is quite possible that some of the issues he wrote about with such passion were not in fact as serious as he thought at the time. But Luke, writing some time later, could take a more detached view of these things, and see them in their proper perspective, both in the life of Paul and in the ongoing experience of the church.

This does not mean that Luke was any less a friend or even a disciple of Paul. A good teacher does not turn out students who are detailed replicas of himself. Instead, he aims to encourage them to develop their own distinctive thinking. And, as we shall see below, the positions that Luke adopts in Acts differ from Paul in the details rather than on the fundamentals.

The real choice for the date of Acts is

between the sixties and the eighties of the first century. But the evidence on the one side is as problematic as that on the other, though the balance of probability seems to favour a date in the eighties, perhaps around AD 85.

The value of Acts

What sort of a book is the Acts of the Apostles? We have occasionally referred to it as a history of the early church, but of course it is not a comprehensive history. There are so many things it does not tell us that it is clearly not the full story of early Christianity. Instead, it is a selective story, drawing attention to those people and movements which Luke believed to be especially significant. In writing his Gospel, Luke had adopted exactly the same procedure. Indeed, none of the New Testament Gospels is a comprehensive account of the whole of Jesus' life. In his Gospel Luke selected those aspects of the life and teaching of Jesus which meant most to him, and in Acts he did

the same thing, picking out those incidents which for him typified the trend of events among the first Christians. He wanted to show how Christianity spread from Jerusalem to Rome, and everything that he records is intended to illuminate that transition. In the process, he omits many things we would like to know. What happened to Peter? And how did James get on in the church at Jerusalem? Or what did the other apostles do? Luke simply ignores these questions because they were not relevant to his purpose.

This means that his story is also an interpretation of the progress of the early church. All history, of course, is an interpretation of past events. When you read the newspaper, you are not getting a 'factual' account of what it describes: you are getting the facts as they were understood by a reporter who was there. Even watching events on television does not enable you to see and to hear exactly what you might have seen and heard had you actually been there, for you can only see and hear what the camera is aiming

On film or television, what we see is dictated by the editorial decision of the person directing the camera. It reflects what he judges to be of significance. Similarly, in the book of Acts, Luke recounts the events which he considers important in the development of the early church.

54

at. There could well be other things taking place just out of sight which would radically alter your whole perception of what was going on. But you have to depend on what the television technicians and editors have decided is important. So when we say that Luke gives us his interpretation of early church history we are not saying anything that would not be true of any kind of second-hand knowledge we may have. We are not suggesting, for example, that Luke simply invented his stories. Indeed, if nothing had happened, there would have been nothing to interpret! But what we have in Acts is the way that Luke, from his

the Gospel. In addition to that, he was himself personally present for at least some of the events in Acts (the 'we passages').

● The picture Luke paints of life in the earliest Palestinian churches is consistent with what we would expect. Much of the theology which he attributes to those earliest Christian believers has a far less sophisticated character than the theology either of Paul or of the church later in the first century. For example, Jesus is still referred to as 'the Messiah' (Christ) in Acts 2:36; 3:20; 4:27, and he can be called 'the Servant of God' (Acts 3:13,26; 4:25-30), or even in one instance, 'the

The Roman emperors exacted heavy taxes from both their own people and those in subject provinces. This third-century relief shows the payment of *tributum*, a tax on land and personal property.

own presuppositions and background, saw the history of the early church.

There are in fact a number of reasons for thinking that the picture which we have in Acts is an essentially authentic reproduction of life in the period which it describes:

● In the prologue to his Gospel (Luke 1:1-4) Luke tells us how he worked: he read all that he could find, sifted through it and then wrote his own considered account of what had happened. In the case of the Gospel, we can see how he went about it, for we possess at least one of his source documents (Mark). The way he uses Mark shows that he was a very careful writer, aware of the need to reproduce his sources accurately and without distortion. We have no direct knowledge of his sources for Acts, though it is widely supposed that he relied on written information for his story of early events in Jerusalem and Samaria (chapters 1–9). If so, he would probably take the same care in compiling his story in Acts as he had previously taken with

Son of Man' (a title much used by Jesus himself but found nowhere in the rest of the New Testament except Acts 7:56). The Christians are called simply 'disciples' (for example, in Acts 6:1-7; 9:1, 25-26), and the church itself is 'the Way' (Acts 9:2; 19:9,23; 24:14,22). Professor Norman Perrin describes all this as 'extraordinarily realistic . . . the narratives of Acts are full of elements taken directly from the life and experience of the church'.

● This same realism can be seen in Luke's description of the Roman world and its officials. He always uses the right word to describe Roman administrators and sometimes uses words that would only be familiar to people living in particular cities. Sergius Paulus and Gallio are correctly designated 'proconsuls' (Acts 13:7-8; 18:12). Philippi is accurately described as a Roman colony, ruled by the *Stratēgoi* (Praetors). This is an unusual word to find in a literary source, but it has been discovered on inscriptions, showing that it was the colloquial term used in

Philippi itself (Acts 16:12, 20-22). Thessalonica also has its own name for its rulers, who are called 'politarchs' (Acts 17:8). This title was once thought to be a mistake, because it is not found in Latin or Greek literature. But subsequent archaeological discoveries have shown that Luke was right to describe the authorities at Thessalonica in this way. There are also many other points at which Luke's stories can be shown to depend on direct and reliable knowledge of the Roman world as it actually was at the time he is describing.

● The same concern for authenticity can also be seen in Luke's presentation of the problems of the early church. The only real controversy that appears in Acts is concerned with the relationship of Jewish and Gentile Christians. But this argument soon became less important, and after AD 70 it was of no importance at all, except on a theoretical level. At the time when Luke was writing, other issues were far more prominent: heresy and orthodoxy, and false teaching of various kinds. But he never tries to import the problems of a later day into the story of Acts.

● There is just one point which may at first sight appear to contradict our generally positive evaluation of Luke's trustworthiness as a historian. This is his treatment of Paul. It has been suggested, especially by the German scholar Philipp Vielhauer, that as we read Paul's own letters we sometimes get a different view of Paul's life and teaching from the picture in Acts. And of course Acts does not even mention the fact that Paul wrote letters at all! A number of points need to be mentioned here:

Firstly, Luke's failure to mention Paul's letters is not all that serious. He may quite possibly have regarded them as personal letters, and therefore of no great importance for his own purpose. We must also remember that though we regard Paul's letters as primary evidence for his activity, they are to some extent evidence without a context, and it is therefore easy for us to overestimate their original significance.

More seriously, however, it is pointed out that the sort of things Paul concerns himself with in Acts are usually significantly different from his normal concerns in his letters. But again this is not specially surprising. When Paul wrote letters, he was writing to Christians. But when he speaks in Acts he is usually addressing non-Christians. There has been plenty of speculation about the content of Paul's initial preaching to the Galatians, Corinthians, Thessalonians and others, but we

cannot know for certain what he told them. We can be sure that he would present his message in a different way to engage the attention of the unconverted than he did when trying to correct the errors of those who were already Christians. It is noteworthy that in the only instance when Acts gives us an address to Christians by Paul (Acts 20:17-38), the substance of his message is not materially different from the typical content of his letters. Even the sermon at Athens (Acts 17:22-31) is not significantly different from what he wrote on the same subject in Romans 1:18–2:16.

A third consideration, however, is that significant differences are said to emerge when we get down to what many believe to have been the central feature of Paul's thinking: 'justification by faith'. But this is not a strong argument. It depends on the assumption that 'justification' was in fact the centre of Paul's thinking. Many readers of the New Testament – especially those of the Lutheran tradition – regard this as beyond question. But does the legal theory of justification by faith as conventionally understood really occupy the centre of Paul's thinking? It assumes such large importance in letters like Galatians and Romans only because, either really or potentially, Jewish opponents were in view. But quite apart from that, 'justification' does in fact appear on the lips of Paul in Acts 13:39 (the sermon in the synagogue at Antioch in Pisidia). And though what is said there is certainly not as fully worked out as Paul's arguments in Galatians or Romans, it is not out of keeping with them. Paul's statements are in any case the work of a trained rabbinic theologian. Luke's report of Paul's thinking is the work of an interested layperson. Though it is fashionable nowadays to speak of Luke as a 'theologian', he was not a professional, and he would not have had the same concern for detail that Paul himself no doubt had. John Robinson has rightly drawn attention to the fact that the kind of theology Luke attributes to Paul is exactly what we would expect in the circumstances. He shows his knowledge of key phrases and ideas that Paul used, though he is less interested than Paul in the detailed arguments that could be brought out in their support.

The purpose of Acts

Though he does not address their problems directly, Luke must have hoped that his first readers would learn something from his story to help their own Christian thinking. He may therefore have had at least three primary aims in view:

● Perhaps the main thing that comes out clearly from Acts is the conviction that Christianity is a faith with the potential to change the world. Indeed, through Paul and others it *did* change the world, and the secret of its success was the way in which these first Christians had the power of the Holy Spirit working within them. Luke encourages his readers to follow the example of those who had been Christians before them, and to do for their generation what Paul had achieved in his.

● But then Luke also seems to go out of his way to emphasize that Christianity can have good relationships with the Roman Empire. On the one hand, he commends the Christians to Rome itself, as he stresses that their faith is the true successor of Judaism – and Judaism, of course, was a recognized religion within the empire. But he also encourages his readers themselves to take a positive attitude towards the empire. He emphasizes that its officials are good and upright men, and by implication suggests that a maniac like Nero was the exception rather than the rule.

● In view of what he says at the beginning of his Gospel, we must also take seriously the fact that Luke claimed to be the first historian of Christianity. His two books are addressed to Theophilus in order that he might know the facts about the Christian faith. And the procedure that Luke adopted for compiling his story does suggest that he had a historian's interest in finding out about the past for its own sake. As the church became established as a significant institution in the Roman world, it was important for its members to know their origins and history, and Luke was perhaps the first person to set some of it out in a systematic form.

The presence of uniformed soldiers was a constant reminder to occupied nations of Roman power. Despite the resentment this could cause, Luke advocated a positive attitude towards the empire and its administrators.

The missing apostles

All three synoptic Gospels, together with Acts, list twelve special disciples of Jesus. Yet apart from Peter, James, John and Judas Iscariot, none of them feature prominently in the Gospels, and they are not mentioned at all in the rest of the New Testament. We do not really know what happened to these people, but there are a number of stories about them in early Christian writings outside the New Testament.

Thomas supposedly went to India, where he died as a Christian martyr – though not before he had persuaded a notable Indian ruler and his family to believe in Jesus. The Mar Thoma church in southern India claims that he was its founder, but it is more likely that it was established by other missionaries from the church in Edessa, by the banks of the River Euphrates. Eusebius says that Thomas himself went to Edessa, and perhaps that is why the Indian Christians regarded him as their patron saint (Eusebius, *Ecclesiastical History* 3.1.1).

Andrew is said to have travelled extensively throughout Greece and Asia Minor, even crossing to the northern shores of the Black Sea. His life was allegedly characterized by miraculous deeds, including the resurrection of thirty-nine dead sailors washed up from a shipwreck! But when the proconsul's wife in the Greek city of Patrae became a Christian, her husband was so enraged that he had Andrew crucified on a cross shaped like the letter X. Other legends claim that sometime between the fourth and ninth centuries, his arm-bone was taken by Regulus to Scotland, where Andrew became the patron saint and his cross the national flag.

Thaddaeus is mentioned in the New Testament only by Matthew and Mark. According to Eusebius (*Ecclesiastical History* 1.13), a man of that name was connected with the establishment of the church in Edessa. The story tells how Abgar, king of Edessa, had written a letter to Jesus asking that he be healed of a disease. Jesus replied that after his

Argentinian evangelist Luis Palau travels worldwide preaching to thousands about the new life that Jesus Christ offers.

ascension, Thaddaeus would be sent to heal him. But other traditions connect Thaddaeus with Africa.

Philip and *Bartholomew* feature in stories about their travels around Asia Minor, accompanied by Philip's sister Mariamne. The *Acts of Philip* tell of encounters with dragons and beasts who speak to them, with Philip finally being martyred in Hierapolis. But Clement of Alexandria suggests that he lived to old age. Bartholomew has also been connected with a mission to India.

Matthew is said to have preached in Judea for eight years after the ascension, before going off to Ethiopia and Arabia. According to Papias, he had something to do with the Gospel of Matthew.

James the son of Alphaeus is mentioned in Spanish traditions that tell how Theodorus, Bishop of Iria, discovered his tomb at Santiago in 835, apparently guided there by a star.

Simon the Zealot travelled to England, according to some stories, together with Lazarus and Joseph of Arimathea.

We cannot trust any of these traditions about the 'unknown' apostles. Some of them may conceivably be based on vague recollections of their exploits, but on the whole their stories are just designed to fill in the gaps in the New Testament story, and have no historical value.

2 The Spirit and the letter

THE FIRST people to take the message about Jesus to Rome had probably been involved in the amazing events of the Day of Pentecost in Jerusalem. Visitors from Rome were certainly present on that occasion, and even if they did not return home immediately, we can be sure that it would not have been long before the message of Jesus arrived in their city. In a day when all roads quite literally led to Rome, it was inevitable that Christian believers would soon share their new faith with the inhabitants of the imperial city. The precise circumstances of the gospel's first arrival in Rome is shrouded in mystery. But it was certainly long before either Peter or Paul had ever been there. It is most likely that, as in other cities in the Roman Empire, the Christian message was first taken to the Jewish synagogues in Rome itself. Luke tells us that the Roman visitors to Jerusalem at the festival of Pentecost were 'Jews and Gentiles converted to Judaism', and on their return they would

Acts 2:10-11

Visitors and pilgrims still flock from all over the world to Jerusalem, just as the crowds poured in for that memorable first Day of Pentecost.

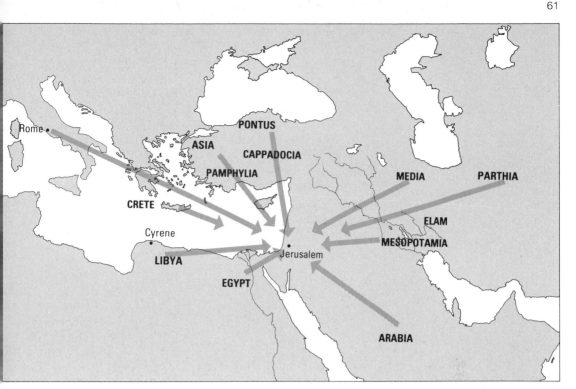

Peter's audience on the Day of Pentecost.

naturally tell their friends how their own lives had been changed because of the preaching of Peter and the power of the Holy Spirit. Their testimony must have been highly effective, for according to Suetonius the Christian claims caused such furious arguments among the Jewish population in Rome that by AD 49 the emperor Claudius had to take steps to restore public order.

Life of Claudius 25.4

The church is born

The very first Roman congregation no doubt took its form from the experiences of the first disciples on the Day of Pentecost, when their hesitating and uncertain trust in Jesus and his promises had been remarkably confirmed by the coming of the Holy Spirit. As a result, they were convinced that they were now experiencing the climax of all God's promises in the Old Testament – and they were also quite sure that the presence of the living Jesus was with them in a unique way. Stephen is the only one whose claim to see the risen Jesus has been recorded for us by Luke. But all these early believers had no doubt at all that Jesus was truly with them. Not all of them could see him literally, as the disciples and others had done for a time after the resurrection. Nor did they all have visionary experiences of one sort or another. But their whole life was revolutionized in such a way that they needed no further argument to persuade them that their everyday experience was a direct result of the power and presence of Jesus in their own lives. Peter, John and others had the power to perform remarkable deeds in the name of Jesus – and, of course, Peter himself was given the unexpected ability to speak in a powerful way to the crowds gathered in Jerusalem.

Acts 2:14-21

Acts 7:55-56

Acts 2:43; 3:1-10

Acts 2:14-39

The Day of Pentecost

The precise nature of the disciples' experience on the Day of Pentecost has been much discussed. Indeed, some scholars believe that it never happened, and that the whole of the story in Acts chapter 2 was intended by Luke to convey some theological lesson rather than to report an actual incident. In his commentary on Acts, Ernst Haenchen suggests that the key to understanding Luke's purpose here is to be found in the fact that Jewish rabbis linked the festival of Pentecost with the giving of the Old Testament Law at Mt Sinai. According to the late second-century Rabbi Johanan, the one voice of God at the giving of the Law had divided into seven voices, and these had then spoken in seventy different languages. That, together with the fact that wind and fire were present both at Sinai and at the events of Pentecost, is said to be enough to explain the picturesque language used by Luke.

But there is no reason to accept this kind of rationalistic explanation of the story in Acts. For one thing, we have no evidence at all to show that the Jewish rabbis linked Sinai and Pentecost before the second century – and that was long after either the alleged event itself or the lifetime of Luke. In any case, it is inherently probable that the disciples would have been in Jerusalem at the time, and that after the unexpected events of the previous Passover they would have gathered in the way Luke describes, apprehensive about what might happen next.

Perhaps they were naively expecting that, after the death and resurrection of Jesus, there was nothing else left except the end of the world. If so, they were in for a surprise. For the new age of which Jesus had spoken did indeed dawn – but not in the way they expected. The life of God himself broke into their own lives, and they were never to be the same again. Speaking of this experience, Peter had no doubt that what had happened to them was what the Old Testament prophet Joel had expected in 'the last days' (Acts 2:17-18).

We cannot of course penetrate the exact nature of their experience. It certainly had some of the common features of visions, as the disciples saw 'what looked like tongues of fire' (but were not fire), and heard 'a noise from the sky which sounded like a strong wind blowing' (but was not the wind). But the result of this experience was clear for others to see: 'They were all filled with the Holy Spirit and began to talk in other languages, as the Spirit enabled them to speak' (Acts 2:1-4). Speaking in tongues, or 'glossolalia' as it is sometimes called, is mentioned elsewhere in the New Testament as one of the gifts of the Spirit (1 Corinthians 12:10; 14:5-25). It is also widely known and practised today. But it is generally agreed that such speaking in tongues is not the speaking of foreign languages otherwise unknown to the speaker, so much as a kind of ecstatic speech, quite different from the form and content of actual languages. Paul contrasted the speaking of ordinary languages with what he called speaking 'the language of angels' (1 Corinthians 13:1), which suggests that he was aware of this difference.

Some scholars, however, have argued that the experience of the Day of Pentecost was not the speaking of tongues, but the speaking of foreign languages. But if that was the case, it is hard to see why some who heard it should have concluded that the disciples were drunk (Acts 2:13), while others heard God speaking to them quite clearly in terms that they could understand. No doubt the explanation for this lies in the fact that what Luke reported he had learned from others who had been there, and whose lives had been changed as a result of what they had heard. And for them, whatever kind of inspired speech the apostles were expressing, there could be no doubt that they were speaking in terms that could easily be understood. For though they began as interested bystanders, these people were themselves caught up by the power of the Spirit and incorporated into this new and dynamic Christian movement.

As a result of all this, the apostles and their converts were so totally dominated by their love for the living Jesus and their desire to serve him that the humdrum concerns of everyday life were forgotten. Instead, the Christians 'spent their time in learning from the apostles, taking part in the fellowship, and sharing in the fellowship meals and the prayers'. They even sold their goods, and pooled the proceeds so they could live as a true community of Jesus'

Acts 2:42

followers. Making money was no longer the most important thing in life. The only things that really mattered were praising God, and taking their life-changing message to other people.

Acts 2:44-47; 4:32-35

The charismatic church

It is hardly surprising that in this situation no one gave much thought to the organization of the infant church. These followers of Jesus were not concerned with appointing leaders or writing a constitution or setting up committees. Nor did it occur to them to establish an army of bureaucrats to direct their worldwide mission from some central headquarters. They already had the only organizing force they needed: the guidance of the Holy Spirit himself.

Acts 4:8; 5:32

Acts 4:31

Acts 5:9

Acts 13:1-3

The Spirit told them what to say in their preaching, and gave them the boldness to say it. When Ananias and Sapphira tried to deceive the church, Peter had no doubt that this was a direct challenge not to himself, but to the Holy Spirit. For the church did not belong to the apostles. It had come into being with the arrival of the Spirit, and the ultimate responsibility of its members was not to each other, but to God. We find the same emphasis throughout the later chapters of Acts. When the church at Antioch in Syria sent Paul and Barnabas off as missionaries, it was acting on the instructions of the Holy Spirit, who spoke directly to the congregation through certain Spirit-filled individuals within it. And this sense of dependence on the Spirit's guidance is perhaps the main characteristic of Paul's work, both in the stories of Acts and in his own writings. This emphasis is so strong in Acts that some readers of the New Testament have preferred to regard it not so much as the 'Acts of the Apostles', but rather 'The Acts of the Holy Spirit'.

Many of us today would regard all this as rather naive. It is certainly not the way that we would go about things. If we wanted to establish some new church today, we would first write a constitution and appoint leaders and an organizing committee, together with all the bureaucratic paraphernalia that seems indispensable to the modern mentality. But this difference of approach underlines a fundamental distinction that must be drawn between the life of the earliest church and what most of us know of the Christian church today.

The start of it all

Luke 24:13-24

For at the beginning, nobody ever sat down and planned to start the church. When Jesus died on the cross, his disciples were for the most part disillusioned and perplexed. This was not what they had expected. Even after the resurrection, they were still apprehensive. The church was not the brain-child of the disciples: it was the work of God. On the Day of Pentecost, God spoke to its founder members and worked among them in such power that they had no option but to respond to his orders. Into the deadness of their own frustration, the Spirit breathed the life of God himself. And as individual disciples experienced the compelling power of the Holy Spirit for themselves, they were drawn together in a fellowship of love and friendship – love for God, love for one another, and love

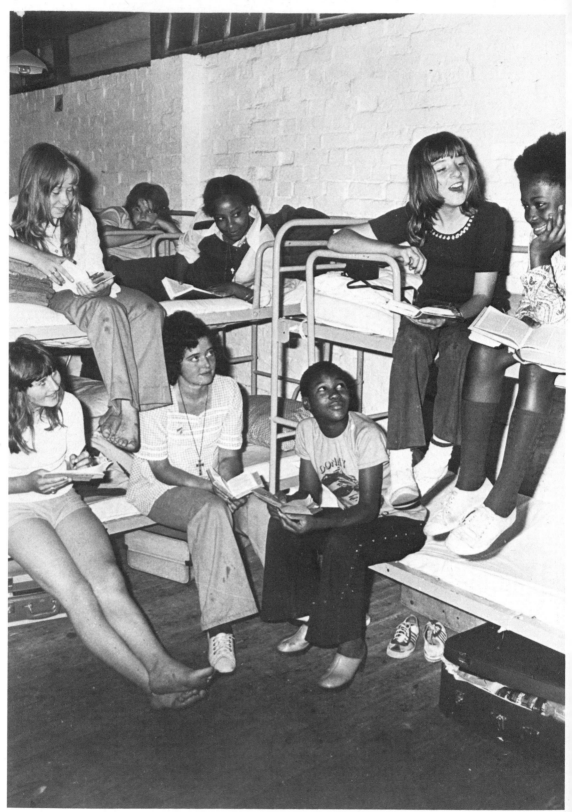

A shared faith in Jesus Christ cuts across barriers of age, sex, class and race.

for the non-Christian world. Their educational, social, economic and political backgrounds were quite diverse, and the only thing they had in common was the fact that through the Spirit, God had changed their lives.

They were bound together as a group not by the fact that they all belonged to the same organization but because they were all inspired by the same Holy Spirit. It is at this point that we can locate the distinctive self-understanding of the early church. To many people today, the Christian church is a kind of religious business enterprise. And like all such secular enterprises, it needs a bureaucracy to make it work. These first Christians, however, saw themselves not as an organization, but as a living organism. Paul expressed this idea most fully when he called the church 'the body of Christ'. What unites Christians, he said, is not the fact that they are all shareholders in the same religious business but the fact that each and every one shares in the life and power of Jesus himself, through the operation of the Holy Spirit in their lives. The Spirit himself was the 'organizing principle' of the church's life, and because of that it was unnecessary for the believers to organize the church themselves. The same kind of argument is used by Jesus when he describes the relationship between Christians and Christ using the imagery of a living plant, with the same source of life filling and energizing all its parts.

Romans 12:4-8; 1 Corinthians 12:12-31

John 15:1-10

This was presumably the concept of the church that the first Christians took to Rome. This so-called 'charismatic' understanding of Christian fellowship was certainly the central feature of Paul's thinking, and we have no reason to doubt that it was the view of other apostles too, including Peter. When Paul wrote to the church at Rome some twenty years after the events of Pentecost, there seems to have been no organized hierarchy. In the final chapter of his letter he seems to imply that there were several groups of Christians there, meeting together in the homes of different individuals in a spirit of mutual love and friendship. Paul mentions a number of people known to him, together with the

Meeting together in homes was a feature of the life of the early church; Christians today also find that this kind of informal setting is important and helpful for sharing their faith.

Romans 16:3-15 names of the people in whose homes these house churches met. Bu he makes no suggestion that any of them had any sort of 'official position among the Christians. Instead, they are all 'Christian brothers and sisters' – just as the followers of Jesus had always been, not only from the Day of Pentecost, but even from the time o Mark 3:33-35 Jesus' own ministry.

The institutional church

Within another forty years, all this had changed quite dramatically Our next piece of evidence from the church at Rome is the early Christian document called 1 Clement. This was a letter sent from the church at Rome to the church at Corinth in about AD 95. It is an especially interesting document, for it lets us see what was going on at that time in two churches that we know about from the New Testament. The church in Corinth had not changed much at all; it was still being torn apart by controversies and arguments of one sort and another. But the church at Rome used a new argument to try to put things right.

Leadership and organization

It suggested that certain of its leaders had special authority, which was vested in them by their position as accredited officials in a church hierarchy: 'The apostles have received the gospel for us from the Lord Jesus Christ. Christ was sent forth by God, and the apostles by Christ. Both these appointments were made in an orderly way, according to the will of God . . . The apostles appointed the first-fruits of their labours to be bishops and deacons for those who would believe. Nor was this a new fashion, for indeed it had been written concerning bishops and deacons from very 1 Clement 42 ancient times . . .'

We can reasonably conclude that by AD 95, these local 'bishops and deacons' in the church at Rome were being thought of as the successors of the apostles – not just metaphorically, but quite literally, for they had the confidence to try and exercise the supreme authority of the apostles, even over the church in the Greek city of Corinth. This impression is reinforced when we notice that in an earlier chapter of 1 Clement, two groups of people are distinguished within the congregation. No longer are they all equal as brothers and sisters in Christ. Instead, we find the notion of 'clergy' and 'laity'. Indeed, there even seem to be two groups of clergy: 'His own peculiar services are assigned to the high priest, and their own proper place is prescribed to the priests, and their own special ministrations devolve on the Levites. But the layman is bound by 1 Clement 40 the layman's ordinances.'

Of course, 1 Clement can only tell us how things were moving in the church at Rome. There is no guarantee that the church in Corinth actually accepted all this when it received the letter, still less that it was itself organized in the same way. But as we look at other Christian literature from the same period, we cannot fail to discern a significant change in the church's self-understanding. There was still a certain degree of admiration for the idea that the church could and should be led by the guidance of the Holy Spirit. But Christians were coming more and more to feel that the church must be organized along more institutional lines.

Ignatius, the bishop of Antioch in Syria at the beginning of the second century, also had something to say on this subject. While he was on his last journey to Rome to face execution, he wrote seven letters to various churches. One of the subjects that he discussed was the relationship between a church and its leaders – and it is clear that, in his view at least, the leaders of the church had a special authority that distinguished them from ordinary church members. There are three distinct types of clergy: the elders or presbyters, the deacons, and over them both, the bishop. The word 'presbyter' has given us the modern word 'priest'. But at that stage there was no thought of sacrifice on behalf of the people in the Old Testament sense. Both bishop and elders should be given great respect, for a *To the Magnesians* 3 person's attitude to them is a reflection of his attitude to God. Indeed, in another letter, Ignatius declares that anyone who agrees with the bishop is a friend of God, while those who disagree with him are God's enemies: '. . . as many as are of God and of Jesus Christ, they are also with the bishop . . . but if any man follows one *To the Philadelphians* 3 who makes a division, he shall not inherit the kingdom of God.'

Again, we must remember that Ignatius was speaking for himself. Many modern readers of his letters have pointed out that he goes to such lengths to defend the status of these religious offices that their significance must have been in some dispute. But nevertheless, it was not long before Christians throughout the world came to accept

It has become the practice for many Christian churches to ordain ministers. This ceremony often includes the laying-on of hands, which was a custom by which the early Christians identified themselves with people who were called to special service.

that this was what the church should be. Instead of the community of the Spirit that it had originally been, the church came to be seen as a vast organization. Instead of relying on the Spirit's direct guidance, it was controlled by a hierarchy of ordained men, following strict rules and regulations which covered every conceivable aspect of belief and behaviour.

By the middle of the second century, the change was complete. At the beginning, the only qualification for membership of the church had been a life changed by the power of the Holy Spirit. Indeed, at the very start there had been no real concept of 'church membership' at all. On the Day of Pentecost, all believers in Jesus were automatically members of the church. There was no need for them to apply to get in, nor could they have opted out, even had they wished to do so. But by the end of the first century things were rather different. Now the key to membership of the church was not to be found in inspiration by the Spirit, but in acceptance of ecclesiastical dogma and discipline. And to make sure that all new members had a good grasp of what that meant, baptism itself was no longer the spontaneous expression of faith in Jesus, as it had *Acts 2:40-42* originally been. Now it was the culmination of a more or less extended period of formal teaching and instruction about the *Didache 7* Christian faith. And in all this, we can see how the life of the Spirit was being gradually squeezed out of the Body of Christ, to be replaced as the church's driving force by the more predictable if less exciting movement of organized ecclesiastical machinery.

The changing church

But why did this happen? Was it just an accident? Or was it a part of some ancient anti-charismatic plot by subversive elements in the church? Or was it perhaps just a good example of the way that any new movement founded by a dynamic leader will eventually become yet another settled institution in its second generation?

We may trace two main reasons for this change in the style of the early church.

Church growth

One of the most impressive features of the early church is the amazing rate at which it grew. Beginning from a handful of people in rural Palestine, within twenty years or less it spread through the whole of the civilized world. All this was achieved with no real organization at all – and yet the very success of this spontaneous world mission was itself to demand some integrated scheme of operation.

At first, no one gave much thought to organization. They already had all the organization they needed. Most of those who became Christians on the Day of Pentecost had been Jews or Gentile converts to Judaism, and they simply accepted and continued in the forms of worship that they already knew and loved. The early chapters of Acts tell how they met with fellow-believers in Jesus, but that was an extra, for they also worshipped in the local synagogues, *Acts 2:46* and even in the temple itself.

But it was not long before the need arose for some kind of organization, however primitive. Stephen came to prominence as a leader among the Hellenist Christians of Jerusalem because they felt they were not getting a fair share in the distribution of church funds. The nature of their complaint implies that the Hebrew Christians were not suffering the same disadvantage – and the fact that the response to the complaint was the establishment of a group of seven men to supervise the distribution of funds to the Hellenists suggests very strongly that there was already in existence a similar group dealing with the needs of the Hebrew Christians.

Acts 6:1-6

We should perhaps not be surprised that these first church 'officials' were appointed to deal with such a practical matter, for the only 'office' known to us in the small group of Jesus' twelve disciples was that of treasurer – a function carried out by Judas Iscariot, sometimes with less than complete honesty. And it is not accidental that the very first stirrings of 'organization' within the early church should be concerned with the same subject. Had not Jesus himself taught that after love to God, love to one's neighbour was the next most important thing? It was certainly one aspect of his message that the early church took very seriously indeed. Its members even sold their goods and property and pooled the proceeds. They were determined to be united with their fellow-believers not only spiritually, but in other more tangible respects too. They all shared one common purse, as well as serving the same Lord.

John 12:4-6; 13:29

Matthew 19:19; 22:39; Mark 12:31, 33; Luke 10:27

Acts 2:44-45; 4:32, 34-35

The 'communism' of the early Jerusalem church

Some scholars, however, have questioned whether this picture of life among the first Christians is authentic. They point out that in Acts 2:44 and 4:32, the believers are said to have shared all their possessions – and yet in a later episode, both Barnabas and Ananias still have property to sell (4:36–5:11). But there is no real contradiction here. The earlier passages themselves make it clear that the members of the Jerusalem church did not dispose of everything at once. Instead, they sold things as the need arose, and then shared the profits with the rest of the Christian community (2:45).

There are no good reasons for doubting the general accuracy of Luke's account at this point. The sharing of goods was nothing new, and was regarded as an ideal by Greek writers, while the Jews were well aware of the need to be charitable. The commune living by the shores of the Dead Sea at Qumran practised a similar sharing of resources, though in this case a convert did not hand over all his possessions until a year after joining the sect.

The distinguishing mark of the Christian 'communism' was its spontaneity. At Qumran, such sharing was carefully regulated by rules, as was the distribution of charity among Jews in general. But Jesus had laid down no hard and fast economic policy for his disciples to follow. Admittedly, he himself lived in relative poverty, and his immediate followers left all they had to join him. When a rich man wanted to become a disciple, he was told, 'Go and sell all you have and give the money to the poor' (Mark 10:21) – and it is difficult not to conclude that Jesus believed a rich person would find it harder to follow him than a poor one (Matthew 19:24). But even the poor could become obsessed with riches, and they too were expected to give away their last coin in the service of God (Mark 12:41-44).

So it is not difficult to understand why these early Christians wanted to share their resources with one another. Yet it does not seem to have been an altogether successful enterprise, for we hear nothing more of such whole-hearted sharing, either in Jerusalem or elsewhere. According to the Marxist historian Karl Kautsky, this is because, after its humble proletariat beginnings, the church soon moved into the middle classes of society, and here the ideals of communistic life were not so attractive. It is certainly true that as the church moved into the wider Roman world, some of its converts came from the higher social classes. But this was not the case in Palestine. Everything we know of the church in Jerusalem suggests that it continued to be poor throughout its existence. The church at Antioch in Syria sent a gift to Jerusalem (Acts 11:27-30), as did Paul's Gentile churches (Romans 15:22-29). Paul twice refers to the Jerusalem church as 'poor' (Romans 15:26; Galatians 2:10), and later Jewish Christians in Palestine called themselves 'Ebionites', which meant simply 'the poor'.

It is more likely that this early experiment in community living broke down simply because the Christians ran out of money. In their enthusiasm, perhaps they had forgotten to balance a sharing of goods with a sharing of labour, with the result that they disposed of the resources they already had, but could find no way of replenishing them.

The excavated buildings of the Essene monastery at Qumran give a flavour of the communal life-style which this religious group sought to put into practice.

Though this primitive kind of communism was not to be typical of the church when it spread to other parts of the Roman Empire, the sharing of goods to a greater or lesser degree was always part and parcel of the Christian gospel. We have already noticed the generosity of the church at Antioch and the Gentile Christians of Greece and Asia Minor. Jesus' emphasis on loving one's neighbour was taken seriously throughout early Christianity. The New Testament is full of exhortations to do just that in many detailed ways – while by the end of the first century, the church was also acting as an employment agency for unemployed Christians.

Acts 11:27-30; Romans 15:26

Didache 12

Obviously, as the church got bigger, the demand for such services increased enormously – and as a result, the co-ordination of aid began to demand more organization than it had required at first. Of course, people performing these jobs were not doing the work of the later 'clergy'. They had no control over worship, and their very existence was more a matter of convenience than anything else. Some translations of the New Testament confuse their role by calling them 'deacons'. But they were not 'deacons' in any modern sense of the word. They had no authoritative position in the church. Quite the opposite: they were the church's servants (the real meaning of the Greek word from which 'deacon' is derived).

But were there others who were formally recognized leaders with responsibility for the regulation of worship and belief in the early churches? This is a highly debatable question. Professor Ernst Käsemann has done more than any other modern scholar to enlighten us on Paul's understanding of church order, and he concludes in effect that there was none. At least, there was no bureaucracy as such. Instead, an individual's usefulness in the church was determined directly by his or her endowment with the Spirit. Even the apostles, he claims, had no authority just because they were apostles. They had authority only in so far as the Holy Spirit gave it to them. So even Paul himself was just 'one charismatic among many', and the whole notion of people being specially appointed to a position of authority was quite foreign to Paul's thinking. Instead, all those who had received the Holy Spirit – and it was impossible to be a Christian without that – were 'office-bearers' in the church. The radical Roman Catholic theologian, Hans Küng, accepts much of what Käsemann has to say at this point, as also does the more conservative Dutch theologian Hendricus Berkhof. Applying all this to the modern scene, he writes: 'taking the charismatic structure of the church seriously would put an end to clericalism and a church ruled by ministers.'

There is a great deal of truth in all this, and Professor Käsemann has undoubtedly penetrated to the radical centre of Paul's thinking in a way that few other students of the New Testament have been able to do. At the same time, we need to remember that Paul's charismatic understanding of leadership did not lead to a free-for-all in the church. Paul makes it quite clear that a Spirit-directed leadership will itself involve a certain limitation of the work of any given individual within a church, for not every Christian is equipped by the Spirit to perform the same tasks. When Christians are prepared together to obey the Spirit, he himself will produce a situation in which 'everything must be done in a proper and orderly way'.

It is not inconsistent with this for Paul to refer elsewhere to specific leadership functions within various churches. The church at Philippi has its church leaders and helpers, while Paul's letter to the Thessalonians also mentions 'those who work among you, who guide and instruct you in the Christian life'. But it is certain that such people owed their position not to some formal act of ordination (as later), but simply to their endowment with the Spirit.

When we turn to the church in Jerusalem, we get a slightly different picture. There, James seems to be very much a man in charge of the church, though no doubt he was guided and assisted by others ('the apostles and elders'). Later Christian traditions credit him with having been the first 'bishop' of Jerusalem, and though they may well be exaggerated it seems likely that he owed his position to some sort of hierarchical arrangement.

We know very little of the formal organization of other churches during the New Testament period. Even the church at Rome is something of a mystery. When Paul wrote to it, he mentioned no leaders at all, though his list of house churches tends to suggest that

1 Corinthians 12

1 Corinthians 14:40

Philippians 1:1

1 Thessalonians 5:12

Acts 15:6, 22

Romans 16:3-15

Acts 20:17; Hebrews 13:7, 17, 24;
James 5:14; 1 Peter 5:1-5

its organization was much more like the earliest churches in Jerusalem than the later congregation led by James. Books like 2 Peter, 1 John and Jude mention no leaders at all, while others speak vaguely of 'leaders', 'elders' or 'shepherds' but without explaining their functions.

Walter Bauer has suggested that churches in different parts of the Roman Empire developed in different ways and at different speeds, and no doubt this applied to their forms of organization just as much as to their theological development. But we can be quite sure of two things. In the first century, the Christian churches had a

In the tradition of many 'heresies' down the years, Sun Myung Moon, founder and leader of the Unification Church or 'Moonies', claims to have received special revelations from God, though his teaching directly contradicts the Bible.

very loose and diverse form of organization. And that 'of official Christian priests we must honestly admit that there is in the New Testament not the faintest whisper' (R. P. C. Hanson).

Heresy

The single most important factor that led to the development of a well-organized and disciplined church in the second century was the emergence of heresy of various kinds.

The charismatic view that we find in the early chapters of Acts and in Paul had always been open to abuse. That was clearly part of the trouble that Paul had to deal with in the church at Corinth. As long as Christians were truly led by the Spirit, then things could be expected to work smoothly. But the unscrupulous could easily manipulate such a situation for their own ends. It was all too easy for a person's own ideas and selfish motives to be put forward as the Spirit's guidance – and it was correspondingly difficult for others to prove that someone claiming the Spirit's guidance did not actually have it. Paul believed that the Holy Spirit would lead Christians to do only those things that were compatible with the way Jesus himself had lived – producing the 'fruits of the Spirit', especially that supremely Christian virtue, love. But even this was not enough to control the 'pseudo-charismatics' in Corinth. Paul's own position as an apostle was itself called into question, for others were claiming that by the power of the Spirit they were 'super apostles', and their revelations were more spectacular than his.

Galatians 5:22-26
Romans 13:8-10; 1 Corinthians 13

2 Corinthians 11:1-15

Similar arguments are to be found in the background of the letters of John. Wandering teachers claiming the inspiration of the Holy Spirit were not only scandalizing other Christians by their behaviour, but were also putting forward theological ideas that the church and its leaders found unacceptable. But how could Christians deal with such people? In the earlier period the apostles had been the final authority. But as they died, the problem became more difficult. Fringe groups such as the Gnostics were gaining ever more ground, and it soon became clear to those in the mainstream of the church that it was no longer sufficient just to assert that they

1 John 4:7-21
1 John 4:1-6

The early Christians had to meet the challenge posed by heretics by defining more precisely what they believed and by basing their everyday lives on those beliefs.

had the Holy Spirit – for their opponents were making exactly the same claim. Faced with such problems, the church had no alternative but to begin a radical rethinking of its position. What did it believe? How could it be sure of knowing where to get authoritative guidance? And how could it ensure that the church in the second century would follow the guide-lines laid down by Jesus and his apostles at the very beginning? To try and find the answers to these questions, the church began to reassess its life in four main areas:

● *Beliefs*. The Christians of whom we read in the early chapters of Acts had not been too concerned to set out their beliefs in any sort of systematic way. That is not to say they had no theology. Jesus himself had claimed the title 'Son of Man', and in the early chapters of Acts we find him identified as the 'Servant of God' as well as 'the Messiah'. Because of their own experience of the coming of the

Acts 3:13, 26; 4:27, 30
Acts 2:31, 36; 3:18, 20; 5:42; 8:5

Acts 2:36; 7:59-60;
1 Corinthians 16:22

Holy Spirit, they had no hesitation in associating Jesus with God, and giving him the title 'Lord', the name of God in the Old Testament. Of course, they also knew that Jesus had been a real person who lived in Galilee and died on a Roman cross. But they were not concerned with defining their beliefs about Jesus more precisely. The kind of theological reflection that later led to dogmas about Jesus' 'divinity' or 'humanity' seemed both irrelevant and unnecessary.

However, when other people came along with claims that Jesus had been only partly divine, or not really divine at all, the church was faced with a challenge. It was not a new challenge, for Paul had already met something of the sort in Corinth. Perhaps that is one reason why he wrote his letter to Rome not long after that – as a kind of summary and exposition of his own Christian thinking. But after Paul's death, the problem became more acute. 1 John was written to counteract views of this kind, and we shall examine the precise nature of these Gnostic or Docetic beliefs in chapter four. The fact that there were people who called themselves followers of Jesus but had distinctive ideas about his significance meant that everyone in the church had to do some hard thinking, to try and define more precisely what they really believed.

But where could they find their beliefs? The Gnostics and their associates had their own books, and many of their documents are still known to us today – books such as the *Gospel of Thomas*, the *Gospel of Philip*, the *Gospel of Truth* and many others allegedly containing secret teaching given by Jesus to some of his disciples. Up to this point, much of the church's teaching had been passed on by word of mouth. Though most of the New Testament books were in existence by the end of the first century, almost all of them had been written for specific situations in particular churches, and, with the possible exception of the letters of Paul, they had not been gathered together in any sort of permanent collection. Some church leaders, like Papias, still preferred the spoken word to what they could read in books. But the majority felt that the time had come to try and decide exactly what they did and did not believe.

● *Worship.* In the earliest days, the Christians met together every day, and their worship was spontaneous. This seems to have been regarded as the ideal, for when Paul describes how a church meeting should proceed, he depicts a Spirit-led participation in

1 Corinthians 14:26-33

worship by many, if not all members of the church. No doubt this was the natural way to proceed at a time when the church generally met in someone's house. But as churches got bigger it was no longer possible for Christians to meet in this informal setting.

Then there was also the fact that anyone had the freedom to participate in such worship. In the ideal situation when everyone was truly inspired by the Holy Spirit, this was the perfect expression of Christian freedom. But it was also accompanied by the danger that those who were out of harmony with the church's beliefs and outlook could also use this freedom to pervert the faith of the church. Because of this it became necessary to ensure that those who led the church's worship could be relied upon to be faithful to the Christian message as it had been delivered by Jesus and the apostles. By the end of the first century a fixed form of service was in existence for the Lord's Supper, and other forms of Christian worship were also becoming less open than they had been. Not everyone welcomed this. Indeed, the *Didache* itself asserts that the ministry of Spirit-inspired speakers should not be curtailed in the interests of a formal church order. But in the face of growing threats from fringe groups in the church it was inevitable that this should happen eventually, in order to preserve the integrity of the Christian faith.

Didache 9, 10, 14

● *Authority.* If the conduct of worship is to be controlled so as to exclude undesirable elements, two groups must be created within the church: those with the authority to conduct its worship, and those without such authority. It is important to realize that the movement towards a more authoritarian church hierarchy also originated in the fight against unacceptable beliefs. At a time when Gnostics were claiming a special authority because of their alleged

The uninhibited style of worship of a 'charismatic' congregation aims to recapture the Spirit-led freedom of expression in the early church.

endowment with the Spirit, it was important for the mainstream church to have its own clear source of power. It was of little practical use for the church's leaders to claim – even if it may have been true – that they, rather than their opponents, were truly inspired by the Spirit. They needed something more than that – and they found it in the apostles. In the earliest period, supreme authority had rested with them. So, they reasoned, anyone with recognized authority in the church must be succeeding to the position once held by the apostles. They were the apostles' successors, and could trace their office back in a clear line of descent from the very earliest times. They stood in an 'apostolic succession'.

Church growth and heresy were undoubtedly the major reasons for the changing pattern of church life at the end of the first century. But others have claimed to find different reasons for this change, and we must give some consideration to two of their suggestions:

Social change The sociologist Max Weber has argued that any group started by an inspiring leader will inevitably change after his death. As his followers try to adapt his charismatic life-style to the normal concerns of everyday life, the structures they create will inevitably become more institutionalized. This happens for a number of reasons, according to Weber, but economic interests are the most significant. The original leader's close associates subsequently become his official representatives. They therefore have a vested interest in developing an organization, and setting themselves up as a privileged hierarchy with the main job of other members of the movement being to pay their wages.

In the course of this process, the dynamic inspiration of the original leader is lost, and his charisma is changed into a more tangible quality that can be handed on from one holder of an office to another.

There can be no doubt that this is what has happened in the church. Hans Küng has criticized the church and its structures for precisely these reasons. And they are not entirely absent from the New Testament. For example, in 1 Timothy we find the reception

1 Timothy 4:14 of spiritual gifts identified with the act of ordination to an office – and that is a notion that has been widely held in the church ever since. But the odd thing is that it should have taken so long for this new development to happen. The early church became fully institutionalized not in the first generation after Jesus, but in the second and third generations.

Up to that point, the experience of the church runs contrary to what we would expect on Weber's sociological theory. Though Jesus was undoubtedly what he would call a 'charismatic leader', the church also had elements of institutionalism from the start. For example, it observed the Lord's Supper as an exclusive community meal. It practised baptism of its converts, and it was conscious of having traditions to hand on to future generations. Its leaders had great authority, and were, at least on some occasions, paid by other church members. But there was one conviction that prevented the church developing into an organization existing for the sole benefit of its leaders. This was the universally-held belief that Jesus was not in fact dead, but alive – and continuing to work among his followers through the power of the Holy Spirit.

For as long as the church saw itself as the community founded by the Holy Spirit, this state of affairs could continue. But once it became suspicious of the exercise of charismatic gifts (because of their misuse), the living presence of Jesus became more of a dogma than a living reality – and it was a short step from that to the institutionalized church. There is no doubt that sociological analysis is helpful in explaining the course of later church history, and also certain aspects of the life of the earliest churches. But when we look for an explanation of the change from a charismatic to an institutional church, the main reasons lie elsewhere.

Frustrated hope

It has also been argued that the loss of the hope in the future return of Jesus (*parousia*) led to this change in the church's structure. Professor Käsemann has laid great emphasis on this. Jesus and the first Christians, he claims, had a vivid expectation of God's coming intervention in history. Jesus himself declared that God's new society would soon come with power, and after his resurrection the disciples lived in daily expectation of the return of Jesus himself in glory. But of course, nothing happened – and so they had to come to terms with the fact that the world was going to continue as it had always been. As a result, they needed a visible and tangible form of organization.

Mark 9:1

Others, of course, have argued that when Jesus spoke of the coming new society he was speaking of a spiritual experience that his disciples could enjoy here and now. This whole issue is examined in considerable detail in the companion book to this, *Jesus and the four Gospels*, and it is suggested there that both these elements can be found in the teaching of Jesus: God's new society had already arrived in the person of Jesus himself, but its complete fulfilment was yet to come in the future.

Naturally, different groups in the early church found different parts of this message more attractive than others. The Christians in the Greek city of Thessalonica became so excited about the fact that Jesus was to return that they gave up work in order to concentrate on preparing for this great event. But Paul rebuked them for this. Though he shared their sense of anticipation, he was quite sure that scaremongering and imaginative speculation was not the way Christians should behave. He reminded them in the words of Jesus himself that 'The day of the Lord will come as a thief comes at night'. In the meantime, Christians should be good citizens, work for their living and encourage and help other people. That is the way they will be ready for the coming of Christ.

1 Thessalonians 4:13–5:11

1 Thessalonians 5:2

Despite Paul's reticence in making pronouncements on such matters, many people still find it possible to believe that he was

The early church recognizes the New Testament

AD 100

AD 200

AD 250

All dates approximate

Different parts of our New Testament were written by this time, but not yet collected and defined as 'Scripture'. Early Christian writers (for example Polycarp and Ignatius) quote from the Gospels and Paul's letters, as well as from other Christian writings and oral sources.

Paul's letters were collected late in the first century. Matthew, Mark and Luke were brought together by AD 150.

New Testament used in the church at Rome
(the 'Muratorian Canon')

Four Gospels
Acts
Paul's letters:
   Romans
   1 & 2 Corinthians
   Galatians
   Ephesians
   Philippians
   Colossians
   1 & 2 Thessalonians
   1 & 2 Timothy
   Titus
   Philemon

James

1 & 2 John
Jude
Revelation of John
Revelation of Peter
Wisdom of Solomon

New Testament used by Origen

Four Gospels
Acts
Paul's letters:
   Romans
   1 & 2 Corinthians
   Galatians
   Ephesians
   Philippians
   Colossians
   1 & 2 Thessalonians
   1 & 2 Timothy
   Titus
   Philemon

1 Peter
1 John

Revelation of John

To be used in private, but not public, worship
The Shepherd of Hermas

Disputed
Hebrews
James
2 Peter
2 & 3 John
Jude
The Shepherd of Hermas
Letter of Barnabas
Teaching of Twelve Apostles
Gospel of the Hebrews

AD 300

AD 400

**New Testament used
by Eusebius**

Four Gospels
Acts
Paul's letters:
  Romans
  1 & 2 Corinthians
  Galatians
  Ephesians
  Philippians
  Colossians
  1 & 2 Thessalonians
  1 & 2 Timothy
  Titus
  Philemon

1 Peter
1 John

Revelation of John
(authorship in doubt)

**New Testament fixed
for the West by the
Council of Carthage**

Four Gospels
Acts
Paul's letters:
  Romans
  1 & 2 Corinthians
  Galatians
  Ephesians
  Philippians
  Colossians
  1 & 2 Thessalonians
  1 & 2 Timothy
  Titus
  Philemon
Hebrews
James
1 & 2 Peter
1, 2 & 3 John
Jude
Revelation

**Disputed but
well known**
James
2 Peter
2 & 3 John
Jude
To be excluded
The Shepherd of Hermas
Letter of Barnabas
Gospel of the Hebrews
Revelation of Peter
Acts of Peter
Didache

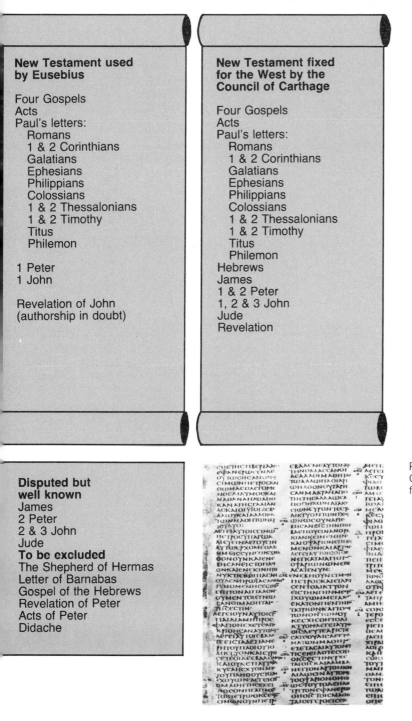

Part of the last chapter of John's
Gospel in Greek, from the
fourth-century *Codex Sinaiticus*

obsessed with nothing but the supposedly imminent end of the world. Professor Käsemann describes Paul quite unjustifiably as 'a possessed man pursuing a feverish dream'. Paul was nothing of the kind, nor were the other leaders of the early church. Of course they believed that Jesus would return one day. But they were also quite sure that in an important sense, Jesus was already with them: in the person of the Holy Spirit.

Romans 8:18-27; 2 Corinthians 5:1-5

In other words, we find exactly the same tension in Paul between present and future as we have already seen in Jesus. In every letter he wrote, Paul gave instructions for Christian behaviour in a settled period of church life. Had he supposed that it was all to come to an abrupt end, such instructions would have been quite unnecessary.

Ephesians 2:1-5; Colossians 2:13

He describes the *present* experience of Christians as 'eternal life', and John uses the same expression. For him, 'eternal life' is not just a life that goes on forever in the future. More significantly, it is the life of God as it can be experienced by Christians here and now in the present.

John 4:23; 17:3

With this kind of outlook, the non-occurrence of the second coming of Jesus would hardly be a problem. But there is one New Testament writing where it seems to be taken more seriously. This is 2 Peter. Here, the writer explains the apparently unexpected delay in the coming of Jesus by the observation that 'There is no difference in the Lord's sight between one day and a thousand years'. But we ought to note that the problem had occurred here because unbelievers had raised it, mocking the church by saying,

2 Peter 3:8

2 Peter 3:4

'He promised to come, didn't he? Where is he?'

Perhaps the issue would never have arisen otherwise – though it certainly became more important to Christians at a later period. Eventually the prospect of a future return of Jesus was lost altogether, and theologians were content to think of the church itself as the new society which Jesus had promised. But this was long after the New Testament period, and the disappearance of a future hope was not the cause of the church's institutionalization, but was one of its results.

In the final analysis, the church became an institution not out of conviction but out of practical necessity. It is easy to look back with hindsight and to imagine that the problems of heresy and church growth could have been tackled in some other way that would have been less inhibiting to further development. But there can be no doubt of the sincerity of the second-century church leaders, nor of their genuine regret that because of excess and abuse, the charismatic ideal was no longer a practical way forward.

Putting the New Testament together

To establish their position, Christians had to decide which books contained an authoritative statement of the church's beliefs, and it was thinking on this subject that eventually led to the collection of our twenty-seven New Testament books as having supreme authority. This collection is often called the 'canon' of the New Testament. The word 'canon' here comes from a similar Greek word meaning 'a measuring stick': the New Testament was to be an accurate measure by which all theological and doctrinal viewpoints could be tested.

From our modern perspective, we

might suppose that somebody in the early church actually sat down and decided which books would form a part of this special collection. But it did not happen like that. The books of the New Testament were not accorded a special authority overnight, and in fact it was well into the fourth century before an actual list of books was drawn up. We can trace four stages in this process:

● Right from the earliest times, Christians gave special authority to certain collections of teaching. The Old Testament, for example, was regarded as sacred Scripture by the New Testament writers. And the sayings of

remember that all the letters in the New Testament were written to specific people for specific purposes, but they do nevertheless contain indications that their authors felt a special authority attached to their words (see, for example, Galatians 1:7-9). By the time 2 Peter was written, Paul's letters at least were regarded very highly, and could be classed as 'Scripture' (2 Peter 3:16).

● When we move beyond the first century, into the period of the so-called 'Apostolic Fathers' (people like Ignatius, Clement of Rome and Polycarp), we find a similar situation. These writers clearly respect many of the New

Through the centuries, as with this 'chained Bible', the Bible has had a place of great importance in the lives of Christians: it is the source-book for belief and behaviour.

Jesus also had a special place in their thinking. But in the very earliest times we find no fixed and clearly-defined body of such teaching. We can see this from the fact that the New Testament occasionally refers to sayings of Jesus that are not contained in the Gospels (see Acts 20:35), and then we also have to take account of the second-century collections of sayings of Jesus, some of which are almost certainly genuine (see *Jesus and the four Gospels*, pages 185-86). The fact that there are four Gospels in the New Testament instead of just one also shows that there was no idea of a fixed and exclusive collection of Jesus' teaching, and John 21:25 mentions many other sayings and deeds of Jesus not included in his Gospel, but no doubt known to some of his readers in one form or another.

The apostles themselves had considerable authority, and their writings were highly respected. We must

Testament books. But they do not regard them as 'Scripture'; in addition, they also valued many other Jewish and Christian writings.

● This state of affairs received a serious challenge from Marcion. In about AD 150, this individual left the church at Rome and declared that he had found a new message. This message had allegedly been given in secret by Jesus to the twelve disciples. But they had not preserved it intact, and so its secret was given to Paul. To prove all this, Marcion made a list of sacred books. This list included only one Gospel (identical with none of the New Testament Gospels, but not too different from Luke), together with ten letters of Paul.

At about the same time there was an explosion of other heretical groups, all of which had their own sacred books. And it was not long before the leaders of the church began to write their own lists.

Towards the end of the second century, Irenaeus, Bishop of Lyons in France, had a kind of 'canon' of New Testament books. He also laid down a rough test for deciding the relative value of different Christian books, suggesting that those of most value were connected with the apostles themselves (*Against Heresies* 3.11.8). This principle, applied by Irenaeus to the Gospels, was refined and extended in the years that followed, and in the third century the church historian Eusebius listed in his *Ecclesiastical History* 3.25.1-7 three different categories of Christian writings: those that were certainly authoritative (the four Gospels, Acts, the letters of Paul, 1 Peter, 1 John and Revelation); those that were certainly not (*Acts of Paul, Shepherd of Hermas, Apocalypse of Peter, Epistle of Barnabas, Didache, Gospel according to the Hebrews*); and those whose status was disputed (James, Jude, 2 Peter, 2 and 3 John).

● Eventually in the fourth century, we find an actual list of authoritative scriptural books, from Athanasius in the eastern section of the church (AD 367), and from the Council of Carthage in the western part of the church (AD 397), and the books they listed are the twenty-seven books of our New Testament. But, of course, they did not gain their authority then. These books had already been widely used and highly regarded for centuries by then, and the decisions made in the fourth century were simply the formal acceptance of a state of affairs that had existed for practical purposes for many years before that.

3 The church and its Jewish origins

WE SHALL never fully understand the story of the early church if we forget that the Christian movement had its origins in the Jewish religion. Jesus was a Jew, as were all his original disciples. Most if not all of the converts on the Day of Pentecost were Jews, but even in the earliest days of the Jerusalem church people like Stephen were asking whether Christianity was a part of Judaism, or whether it was something distinctive and new. These questions became more pressing once Paul and others had moved out into the wider world to take the good news about Jesus to people with no Jewish connections. Yet, though he regarded himself as the 'apostle to the Gentiles', wherever Paul went he always took his message first to the Jewish synagogue. As a result, many of the issues dealt with in his letters have a distinctively Jewish flavour – questions about the Old Testament Law, and the nature of Christian belief and behaviour over against Jewish traditions.

Romans 11:13
Acts 13:14; 14:1; 17:1-2

These issues were to become increasingly important for every aspect of the life of the early church, as Christians took over the Jewish scriptures (the Old Testament) as a part of their own authoritative writings. They naturally needed to know what relationship there might be between the message of God in the Old Testament and their own new experience of Jesus and the Holy Spirit. Paul's answer to this question has already been explored in the companion book, *Paul*. But there are other writings in the New Testament which show us how other Christians were tackling these issues. These writings are generally shorter in length than Paul's

The first Christians had to wrestle with the problem of carrying over Jewish traditions into the life of the early church. In modern times, synagogue worship conducted according to ancient traditions helps to reinforce the strong sense of Jewish identity and their links with the past.

letters, and they are also for the most part considerably less complex. But they are no less valuable for that, for they give us direct access to areas of the church's life and thinking that are mentioned nowhere else in the New Testament.

Four books in particular can help us to understand the Jewish dimension in the life of the church: James, Hebrews, 1 Peter and Revelation. They all have a clear orientation towards Jewish interests, but they are not identical. Indeed their very diversity makes them the more useful, for they give us an insight into at least four different aspects of Jewish thought that were taken over and further developed among the first Christians.

Christians and Jewish morality

Judaism had always been deeply concerned with behaviour. In the Roman world, Jewish people were often distinguished not so much by what they thought as by what they did. They circumcised their male children, kept the sabbath day apart and observed complicated laws about food. These were the things that announced to the Romans that the Jews were different. But they were not the only things. For the Jewish people also had a comprehensive code of moral behaviour. Many of the things that were taken for granted in a pagan life-style were avoided by Jews – not just because they were un-Jewish, but because they seemed to be against the Law of God. As Jewish people in different parts of the Roman Empire explained their ancestral faith to other people, they often found that Gentiles

Christians disassociated themselves from the excesses and debauchery of the Roman festivals.

were attracted by their moral standards. After the self-indulgence of Greek and Roman life, many Gentiles found the Jewish way refreshingly simple and disciplined. There must have been many Romans like Cornelius, who actually became adherents to the Jewish religion ('proselytes') – while many more followed the Jewish way of life without necessarily taking up the full burden of the Torah.

Acts 10:1-2

The foundation of Jewish morality had been laid many centuries before in the Old Testament. Besides its concern with matters of religious ritual, the Torah has a strong moral core, in the Ten Commandments and elsewhere (especially Deuteronomy). It was concerned to ensure that worshippers in ancient Israel should carry their religious beliefs over into the affairs of everyday life. As Amos and other Old Testament prophets never tired of pointing out, it was a waste of time to make high-sounding religious affirmations in the temple if they meant nothing in the market-place.

Exodus 20:1-17

Amos 5:21-24; Micah 6:6-8

James

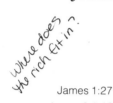
Where does the rich fit in?

The message of Jesus was largely concerned with this theme, and the letter of James is very similar: it emphasizes that religious belief is worthless if it does not affect the way we live. Devotion to God does not end at the door of the church. It only begins there: 'What God the Father considers to be pure and genuine religion is this: to take care of orphans and widows in their suffering and to keep oneself from being corrupted by the world.' The heart of real devotion to God is to love one's neighbour as oneself – and without deeds that will put such sentiments into action, religious faith is worthless.

James 1:27
James 2:1-13

James 2:14-26

Like Jesus, James uses many illustrations to deliver his message. He draws a vivid verbal picture of the apparent splendour of a rich person. Like the flowers whose beauty he tries to copy, his day will soon be over: 'The sun rises with its blazing heat and burns the plant; its flower falls off, and its beauty is destroyed. In the same way the rich man will be destroyed ...' James also turns his attention to the dangers of thoughtless talk. The tongue is just like a rudder, which can steer a ship many times larger than itself; its influence is out of all proportion to its size – and if we are not careful it can make trouble for ourselves and other people. Once a person loses control of his tongue, it can create conditions like a forest fire, which is started by just one small spark but is very difficult to put out.

James 1:10-11; 5:1-6 and Matthew 6:28-30

James 3:1-12

James takes many illustrations from the familiar world of Palestinian agriculture. He condemns the selfishness of the master who refuses to pay his servants a proper wage for a day's work. Jesus had used a similar story to make a rather different point. He told of a master who hired men to work on his vineyard. They started work at different times of the day, so that when the time came for them to receive their wages some of them had only worked for an hour, while others had worked the whole day. But the master gave them all the same wages! Jesus' hearers must have rubbed their eyes with amazement when they heard that, for in their experience employers

James 5:1-6

Matthew 20:1-16

were more likely to treat them in the way James describes. But, of course, Jesus was speaking of a different master: God himself, who is overwhelmingly generous in all his dealings with men and women.

The book of James has no coherent 'argument', any more than Jesus' Sermon on the Mount has a consistent theme. But its message would not be lost on its readers. These people were suffering the kind of discrimination that James mentions, and they are urged to be patient and to trust in God for deliverance. God will keep his promises to his people, and they will be vindicated in the end.

Matthew 5–7

James 5:7-20

A Christian book?

There are many unsolved problems with the letter of James. But two things are quite clear: it is an intensely Jewish writing, and it is

Having faith is a waste of time, James wrote, unless it influences our day-to-day lives and the way we treat other people.

concerned above everything else with correct behaviour. Some have thought it so Jewish that they have doubted whether it is really Christian. Martin Luther had no time for it at all, and he regretted that it had ever been included among the books of the New Testament. By comparison with the other New Testament writings it was, he said, 'a right strawy epistle . . . for it has no evangelical manner about it'. Others have pointed out that James mentions the name of Jesus in only two places, and that when he gives examples for his readers to follow, he chooses Old Testament figures like Abraham, Job, Elijah and even the prostitute Rahab rather than Jesus. No significant facts about Jesus are mentioned anywhere in the book – not even his death and resurrection. Indeed, if we were to look for other books of a similar kind, we would most easily find them in books like Proverbs in the Old Testament and other so-called 'Wisdom' books that were popular with Jewish readers in the time of Jesus.

James 1:1; 2:1

James 2:21-24; 5:11, 17; 2:25

Some have therefore suggested that James was not written by a Christian at all, and that the two references to Jesus were inserted at some later date when Christians became embarrassed by the existence of this apparently Jewish book in their scriptures. But there is no evidence to support this idea. If a later Christian editor had set out to change a Jewish book into a Christian one, he would surely have inserted far more references to specifically Christian ideas than just two mentions of the name of Jesus.

James and Jesus The message of James is in general very much in harmony with the teaching of Jesus. But there is more than just a superficial similarity between them. For there are many detailed points at which James's advice corresponds closely to specific aspects of Jesus' teaching.

Similarities between the teaching of Jesus and James

God is the source and giver of all good gifts	Matthew 7:7-11 James 1:15,17
Christians must pay attention to God's word but also be prepared to put it into practice	Matthew 7:24-27 James 1:22
Christians should share God's mercy with others	Matthew 5:7 James 2:13
Christians should endeavour to make peace in the world	Matthew 5:9 James 3:18
'Love your neighbour as you love yourself'	Matthew 22:39 James 2:8
If this teaching is followed, the true nature of the Christian will be impossible to hide	Matthew 7:16-18 James 3:12
Followers of Jesus can pray to God in the knowledge that he will answer	Mark 11:22-24 James 1:6
God is the only judge and Christians too will have to give an account of their deeds to him	Matthew 7:1-2 James 4:11-12
Christians should make promises that others can accept and trust, because they intend to keep them, instead of trying to emphasize their sincerity by using unnecessary oaths	Matthew 5:33-37 James 5:12

The words of James and the words of Jesus are not *identical* in any of these passages. But the language used and the sentiments expressed are so similar that we can hardly deny there is a connection. The most likely explanation of this is that the writer of James knew these sayings of Jesus in a slightly different form from that now incorporated into the New Testament Gospels. We know that the Gospel materials circulated by word of mouth for some time before they were written down, and the fact that some of this teaching has a more primitive form in James than it does in Matthew suggests that James had access to it at an earlier stage than the writers of the Gospels.

The letter of James

But all this begs an important question. Who wrote the letter of James? And who were its first readers? Most other New Testament books contain some clues that enable us to answer such questions. But in the case of James, we have virtually nothing to go on.

Who was James?

Apart from the mention of a person called James in the opening sentence, the book tells us nothing about its writer, readers or any other event or person. There is no hint as to where James and his readers lived, nor are we told who James actually was. This was a very common name among Jewish people, and a James who is described as 'a servant of God and of the Lord Jesus Christ' could have been any Christian of that name. Similarly, the way the book describes people and their behaviour could apply to many different situations not only in the ancient world, but even today too. It is as pointless to look for the identity of the rich man (James 2:1-4) as it would be to try and find out who the Good Samaritan was (Luke 10:25-37).

Early church traditions give us no more real help. There is no trace of this letter of James in other Christian literature until the end of the second century. Eusebius, the fourth-century church historian, listed it as one of the New Testament books whose value was disputed (*Ecclesiastical History* 3.25.3). But he also added that the same disputed books 'have been used publicly with the rest in most churches', and then he links it with James, the brother of Jesus and leader of the church in Jerusalem (*Ecclesiastical History* 2.23.25). A number of modern scholars believe that, though this statement in Eusebius is much later than the writing of the book of James, it nevertheless contains some truth, and so they regard the book as the work of James of Jerusalem.

If it is necessary to link it with some person by the name of James who is mentioned elsewhere in the New Testament, then there are only two possible candidates: James the disciple and brother of John, and James the brother of Jesus. Of these two, most scholars choose the second, on the ground that James the apostle was martyred in AD 44 (Acts 12:1-3). It is assumed that this date would be too early for the writing of any of the New Testament books, though there is really no evidence to support such an assertion. At the same time, James the disciple does not figure prominently in the stories of the early church in Acts, whereas James of Jerusalem obviously became well-known: he is a central figure in Acts, and also in Paul's writings, and would therefore be in a better position to write to other Christians with no more introduction than his name.

But a number of arguments have been put forward against this idea that James of Jerusalem wrote the letter of James:

● It is written in very good Greek, in an elegant style that shows some acquaintance with Greek literature. But would this be likely if it was the work of a Galilean countryman? This argument once carried considerable weight, because it was believed that Palestine was not so heavily influenced by Greek culture as other parts of the Roman Empire. But we now know that this was not the case, and in an area such as Galilee with a large non-Jewish population a person like James could easily have learned a good deal about the Greek language. At a number of places in the book, the idiom and style of the Semitic languages Hebrew and Aramaic seem to have influenced his writing (2:7; 3:12; 4:13-15; 5:17), which suggests that the writer also spoke one or both of these languages.

● If this book was written by James the brother of Jesus, we might have expected him to make more specific mention of his brother. Since James was not a disciple during Jesus' lifetime, we might even have expected some account of his conversion (1 Corinthians 15:7). But the writer seems to go out of his way to avoid mentioning Jesus directly. There is some weight in this argument, but it really depends on guesswork. If we are not sure of the identity of an ancient author, we can hardly be in a position to judge what he may or may not have been expected to write!

● In James 2:14-26 we have a passage which contrasts faith and actions as the basis of true commitment. Paul also draws the same contrast, especially in his letters to the Galatians and to the Romans, and some scholars have seen in James a deliberate reply to and correction of Paul's viewpoint. If this is the case, then James must have been written after Paul's time, and probably after his views had become a source of controversy – and on any account this must have been long after the death of James of Jerusalem. But there is no reason to suppose either that James knew Paul's writings, or, as some have suggested, that Paul knew of James. Certainly they use the same terminology, but their concerns are different.

● The strongest reason of all for

James draws on imagery from rural life and agriculture for many of his illustrations.

doubting that James of Jerusalem could have written this book is its conviction that true belief should be described in purely ethical terms. We know that James had faced this question over the admission of Gentile converts to the church. Were they to obey the whole of the Old Testament Law or not? While James did not go along with those extremists who insisted that Gentile Christians should become Jews by being circumcised, he did agree that they should observe not only the moral laws of the Old Testament, but also some of the ritual and food laws as well (Acts 15:13-21). Is it therefore likely that he would have written that the 'law of the Kingdom' could be kept by loving one's neighbour (2:8)? There is a fundamental difference between what we know of James from Acts and Galatians (and what we learn from Josephus and other historians) and what we read in the book that bears the same name. In the view of many people, this difference is so crucial that it alone must cast doubt on the alleged connection between the two.

The date

Though this book may well have no connection with James of Jerusalem, a number of facts suggest very strongly that it belongs to an early period of the church's life rather than a later one:

● In its opening sentence, it addresses itself to 'the twelve tribes in the Dispersion' (1:1). Taken literally, of course, that could mean the whole of the Jewish people scattered throughout the world. But it is probably to be seen in the same light as the similar address in 1 Peter 1:1 or Paul's designation of his Galatian readers as 'the Israel of God' (Galatians 6:16). From an early time, Christians saw themselves as the heirs and successors of the people of God in the Old Testament, and it was natural to apply to themselves language that had previously been used of Israel. But, of course, the only period in the church's history when anyone could write to the whole of God's people in this way (as contrasted with 1 Peter, which was addressed only to certain areas) was at

the very beginning of its history – when the church was still essentially Jewish and centred on Jerusalem. Theodor Zahn argues that this points unmistakably to the time after the death of Stephen, but before Paul's travels had begun.

● This is further supported by the fact that there is no sign anywhere in James of a break between Judaism and Christianity. The well-to-do oppressors of the poor (2:6-7) were almost certainly Jews but they are not condemned because of that. All the attention is focussed on their basic selfishness. Moreover, the gathering so vividly described in James 2:1-4 is said to be in 'the synagogue' (2:2). Dr John Robinson believes that this situation is very similar to that described in Acts 4–5 when Jewish aristocrats were oppressing a lower-class proletarian Christian movement.

● The background to much of the imagery of James is clearly Palestinian. The 'autumn and spring rains' of 5:7 meant nothing in other parts of the Roman Empire, while the agricultural practices mentioned in the previous verses are of a type that disappeared for good in Palestine after AD 70, but which were widespread in the days of Jesus.

● There is no evidence anywhere in James of the later practices and problems of the church. Not only is the Jewish/Gentile controversy unknown, but there is no mention of heresy, and no reference to the organization of the church or to doctrinal arguments. Its moral teaching does not include later ethical concerns over the introduction of pagan moral standards into the church. Instead, it is almost exclusively directed to the kind of problems that would occur in a Jewish environment.

Origins

We seem to be faced with two main conclusions. On the one hand, the evidence for associating this book with James of Jerusalem is not all that compelling; but on the other, there are strong reasons for placing it in a very early period of the church's life. So where did it come from, and what was its purpose?

We must recognize that we do not have enough information to give a full answer to that question. But the kind of teaching that we find in James is so similar to that of Jesus himself, and uses so much of the same rural imagery, that it is not unreasonable to suppose it has a similar background. It is not inconceivable that it had its origins among those followers of Jesus who remained in Galilee after the main centre of the church moved to Jerusalem. It is impossible to prove this, of course, for we know next to nothing about such Galilean believers. But the message of James would certainly be especially appropriate to those who were worshipping in the Jewish synagogues of rural Palestine, and at the same time were trying to put into practice what Jesus had taught them. Such people must have been tempted to substitute religious formality for the spiritual realities of which Jesus had spoken – and, as a relative minority, they would also be open to the kind of persecution that James mentions.

If the book originated in such a context, this may also explain why it went unrecognized in the wider church for so long. Its eventual association with an important person like James of Jerusalem would then have been a means of justifying its inclusion in the canon of the New Testament. It could also reflect the possibility that the church in Jerusalem was included in 'God's people in the Dispersion', to whom James was originally despatched at an early stage in the history of the church.

It has been suggested that the writer of James spoke both Hebrew and Aramaic. This Hebrew text from the Pentateuch is accompanied by an Aramaic paraphrase (or *Targum*).

'Faith' and 'works' in Paul and James

When Martin Luther called James 'an epistle of straw', his main reason for doing so was that he believed James's theology was fundamentally different from Paul's – and, since Paul was his hero, he was forced to relegate James to a secondary position. If we compare James 2:24 with Romans 3:28, we can soon see what led him to this conclusion:

● **James 2:24**: You see that a man is justified by works and not by faith alone.
● **Romans 3:28**: For we hold that a man is justified by faith apart from works of the law.

These two statements have every appearance of being mutually contradictory. Not only do they seem to be saying opposite things from each other: they also use exactly the same Greek words to do so! But when we examine them more carefully, and

especially when we place them in their proper contexts, this alleged contradiction becomes much less obvious:

● Though they both speak of 'faith', James and Paul seem to mean rather different things by this word. For Paul, it has almost a technical sense, referring specifically to that belief and commitment to Jesus that characterizes the Christian life. In James, however, 'faith' has a much broader meaning. No doubt specifically Christian faith is not excluded, but it is not the main emphasis. This is on 'faith' as belief in God, as opposed to atheism. James is more concerned with the intellectual acceptance of theological propositions, whereas Paul is exclusively concerned with commitment.

● There is a similar distinction in the way they use the term 'works'. When James mentions 'works', he is referring to the kind of behaviour that naturally stems from commitment to Christ (1:25;

2:8). But the 'works' that Paul writes about are the actions and rituals that were prescribed in the Old Testament Law. Paul refers to things that a person would do in order to gain God's approval. James refers to the things a person will do because he or she already has a living relationship with God through Christ.

● Paul and James were addressing themselves to different practical problems, and this inevitably affected the way they expressed themselves. In Galatians and Romans, Paul was contending against the self-righteousness of people who thought that by keeping the Old Testament Law they could commend themselves to God. So he condemns the keeping of the Law – and in doing so, he echoes the teaching of Jesus (Matthew 5:3; Luke 18:9-14). James, on the other hand, was fighting against the temptation to suppose that right belief is all that matters – and he accordingly emphasizes that doctrines with no practical effect are worthless. Again, he also echoes the teaching of Jesus (Matthew 7:21-23).

Christians and Jewish ritual

1 Kings 8:20-21

Jeremiah 21:1–23:32

Ezra, Nehemiah

The temple in Jerusalem had always held a special place in the life and thinking of Jewish people. Built originally in the time of Solomon, at the height of Israel's political expansion, the temple and all that it represented came to have an almost mystical significance. Even in the dark days just before its destruction by Nebuchadnezzar, king of Babylon, the people of Jerusalem had believed against all the odds that the presence of the temple in their city would somehow save them from invasion. They were wrong, of course, as the prophet Jeremiah was quick to remind them – for they were pinning their hope on an outward form of religious activity instead of on a personal relationship with God himself.

Almost 150 years after Nebuchadnezzar had plundered Solomon's temple, it was eventually patched up and brought back into regular use under the influence of Ezra and Nehemiah. But by the New Testament period it was in the process of being replaced with a structure even more splendid than the original had been. In 20 BC, Herod the Great decided that he would build a temple that would be as impressive as any building anywhere in the Roman world. But he did not live to see it finished. The work was so ambitious and costly that it went on for something like eighty years. The new temple was eventually completed – only to be destroyed shortly afterwards by the Roman general Titus in AD 70.

This was the temple that Jesus and the first Christians knew, and it was a centre of devotion for Jewish believers from all over the Roman Empire. By New Testament times Jewish synagogues had been established in every town or city where there was a Jewish population of any size. But worship in the synagogue was not the same as worship in the temple. The synagogue had originated as a social convenience for Jews living in lands far removed from Palestine. But it was at the temple in Jerusalem that Israel's religious past could be seen in true focus. The worship of the synagogue could incorporate some of the ancient rituals such as circumcision and the old food laws. But it was only in the temple that the rites prescribed in the Old Testament could be carried out in their entirety. Here, the priests still offered sacrifices as they had done for generations past, and the great religious festivals had special significance when celebrated in the temple at Jerusalem.

Overleaf: The temple in Jerusalem occupied a site with a long-established tradition of sacrifice. Temple worship came to an end in AD 70 when the Romans sacked the city; the Moslem Dome of the Rock was built in 691–92 on the same site.

Jews from all over the empire had the ambition to go there and worship in its holy places. The crowds who gathered to hear Peter on the Day of Pentecost were not at all unusual: Jerusalem was the one place that every pious Jew must visit at least once in his lifetime.

But what were the new Christians to think about all this? Gentile believers with no previous connection with the Jewish faith had never thought of the temple at Jerusalem at all. But those who had been Jews before becoming Christians saw it as an important question. For the Torah was not just a compendium of moral instructions. It also contained detailed regulations for the proper conduct of worship. No one seems to have questioned the acceptance of Jewish standards of behaviour in the church. But what was to be done with the ritual of the Jewish religion?

This was a more complex question, for it included not only the role of the temple in Jerusalem, but also the vexed problem of circumcision. That was ultimately solved in favour of those who, like Paul, believed that the Old Testament Law was not directly relevant to the Christian life. But there were many Jewish Christians who not only continued with practices like circumcision but also felt a special affection for the priesthood and ritual of the Old Testament. The first followers of Jesus in Jerusalem had partici-

Acts 2:46; 3:1 pated freely in the services at the temple: it never occurred to them not to do so, and in any case that was where they would find others willing to listen to their new message about Jesus. But as time passed, things soon changed. Many Hellenist Christians felt, like Stephen, that the day of the temple and its rituals was finished altogether. The death of Jesus had now made repeated sacrifices for sin a thing of the past. But the church in Jerusalem seems to have continued to worship in the temple, and was allowed to do so because of its relatively conservative stance on the issue of Gentile Christians. And there were many others who wished to join them. After all, these Hellenist Christians had been born Jews. No one could change that. In addition, their non-Christian compatriots were naturally eager to know where they stood. Did they support and approve of the Jewish way of doing things – or did they, like Stephen, believe that even the temple was now redundant?

Hebrews This is the kind of question that seems to lie behind the New Testament book of Hebrews. The way the author encourages and advises his readers seems to suggest that they were being persecuted in some way. This may explain why the question of Jewish worship had become so important to them: if they were prepared to conform to Jewish practices, life could be a lot easier. The early

Acts 13:50; 14:5,19 chapters of Acts show how antagonistic Jews could make life difficult for Christian believers, and some scholars believe a similar situation is envisaged here. On the other hand, Christians throughout the Roman Empire must have been tempted to try and link themselves to Judaism in some way, especially in times of persecution. For Judaism was a permitted religion under Roman law, whereas Christianity was not.

The writer of Hebrews was quite sure that it was both pointless and unnecessary for Christians to keep the ritual requirements of the Old Testament Law. The message of Jesus is God's final word to men and women. The prophets and others in ancient Israel had spoken in God's name to the people of their own time, but they were all now superseded by Jesus. Even Moses and Joshua were insignificant compared to Jesus, not to mention the angels who according to Jewish tradition had been connected with the giving of the Torah. Jesus was also far greater than Aaron, the archetype of every Jewish priest. Aaron was only an ordinary man, as great a sinner as the rest of the people. But Jesus was the Son of God. Because of his human experience, he understood how people felt when faced with the power of evil. But he was not affected by it, and he could therefore be thought of as 'a great high priest', who has provided 'eternal salvation for all those who obey him'.

Hebrews 1:1-3
Hebrews 3:1–4:13

Hebrews 1:4–2:18

Hebrews 2:17-18; 4:14-15

Hebrews 4:14–5:10

Continuing to write of Jesus under the imagery of the Jewish priesthood, Hebrews goes on to suggest that a more suitable Old Testament illustration of what Jesus had done may be found in the figure of Melchizedek. He is a shadowy figure of whom we know next to nothing. In one of the psalms, the king in Jerusalem is called 'a priest for ever in the line of succession to Melchizedek', and many Christians have applied this description to Jesus. He also appears briefly in a story about Abraham. But the writer of Hebrews uses the obscurity of the Old Testament record to his own advantage. Since 'There is no record of Melchizedek's father or mother or of any of his ancestors; no record of his birth or of his death', he must be 'like the Son of God', who is similarly timeless. He also draws attention to the fact that Abraham had recognized the greatness of this priestly figure, long before Aaron and his descendants had ever been heard of. If the great ancestor of the Jewish nation had himself paid homage to Melchizedek, then that in itself was enough to demonstrate the superiority of his position over the later priestly line descended from Aaron. For since Aaron was as yet unborn, he was at least potentially present in Abraham's body when he met Melchizedek. If further proof of Jesus' supremacy was needed, there was always the fact that the Old Testament priests died and were succeeded by others, while Jesus, like Melchizedek apparently, lived for ever.

Hebrews 5:11–7:28

Psalm 110:4

Genesis 14:17-20

Hebrews 7:3

The sacrifice of Jesus

The precise form of the author's argument may elude most of us today. But for him the point of it all is simple: 'we have such a High Priest, who sits at the right of the throne of the Divine Majesty in heaven. He serves as High Priest in the Most Holy Place, that is, in the real tent which was put up by the Lord, not by man.' Everything that had been achieved on a temporary basis through the rituals of Old Testament worship – first in the 'tent' (or tabernacle), then in the temple – had now been achieved permanently by Jesus. The sacrifices offered by the Old Testament priesthood had to be repeated, because they could only account for past wrongdoing. But the sacrifice of Jesus (himself, on the cross) had more far-reaching

Hebrews 8:1-2

Hebrews 9:25-28

Hebrews 9:14

Hebrews 10:9

Hebrews 10:29

Hebrews 6:4-8

Hebrews 10:39

Hebrews 11:1-38
Hebrews 11:39-40

Hebrews 12:1-11

Hebrews 12:14; 13:1-21

Hebrews 13:21

consequences. Not only was it the basis on which men and women could be forgiven and accepted by God, but the divine power released by it could also set them free from 'useless rituals, so that we may serve the living God'.

Now, 'God does away with all the old sacrifices and puts the sacrifice of Christ in their place'. Because of that, those who are tempted to go back and take part in the old rituals of Judaism are actually denying the effectiveness of what God has done in Jesus. They are 'despising the Son of God', and insulting the Holy Spirit. They have effectively joined with those who reject Jesus, and God has no time for such people. To turn back to Jewish ways is to be lost, but those who trust in God and accept what he has done for them in Jesus will find true and lasting salvation.

All this is strong stuff. But our author was convinced that it was nothing new, for he goes on to list a 'large crowd of witnesses' taken from the Old Testament and Jewish history, whose experience of God can bear this out. These people will receive the same reward as faithful Christians, and their story should be a lasting encouragement to Christians to get their priorities right and to keep their eyes firmly fixed on Jesus alone as their example and inspiration. To do this, they must live at peace with others and show love for their fellow-Christians, as well as members of their own families. By doing so, they will please God and he himself will 'provide you with every good thing you need in order to do his will'.

Hebrews: author, readers and date

According to Eusebius, the third-century Church Father Origen wrote of this book, 'only God knows the truth as to who actually wrote this epistle' (*Ecclesiastical History* 6.25.14). Some translations and versions of the Bible give it the title, 'The epistle of Paul to the Hebrews'. But these words are not original, and it is highly unlikely that this book has anything to do with Paul:

● For one thing, it is not really an epistle at all. When Paul wrote letters he always followed the normal practice of Greek letter-writers (see *Paul*, page 48). He also leaves us in no doubt as to who his readers were and what has caused him to write to them. But Hebrews is not addressed directly to anyone, and the only possible reason for supposing it to be a letter of some sort is the inclusion of what appears to be a personal greeting after the benediction with which the book closes (13:22-25). Some have suggested that this section was added later, to make Hebrews look like one of Paul's letters. It has even been suggested that Paul himself added the news of Timothy given in 13:23 to a book that Timothy had originally written. But there is nothing to support either of these conjectures.

● The language and style of Hebrews is in any case totally different from that of Paul's writings. Hebrews has just about the best Greek style of any New Testament book, and reaches a far higher literary standard than Paul could ever aspire to. Even Origen noticed this: 'the character of the diction of the epistle entitled "To the Hebrews" has not the apostle's rudeness in speech . . . that is, in style. But that the epistle is better Greek in the framing of its diction, will be admitted by everyone who is able to discern differences of style' (Eusebius, *Ecclesiastical History* 6.25.11-12).

● The concerns of Hebrews are also quite different from Paul's interests. If, as many believe, it was written primarily for the benefit of Jewish Christians, then Paul is unlikely to have written it in any case. But even if it was written for Gentiles, its interest in the Torah is quite different from Paul's. Above all else, Paul emphasized the *moral* demands of the Old Testament Law. The ritual of tabernacle, priests and sacrifices which is so important in Hebrews did not concern Paul.

We can be quite sure that Paul did not write Hebrews. But it is not easy to decide who did. There is so little specific reference to people and events that the most diverse characters have been suggested, all with more or less equal plausibility: Barnabas, Apollos, Timothy, Aquila and Priscilla, and Luke have all been put forward as possible candidates. In reality, we are no nearer to a solution than Origen was. But we can discover a number of facts about the unknown author from what he has written:

● He did not belong to the same group as the apostles. Explaining how the Christian message had reached him, the writer comments: 'The Lord himself first announced this salvation, and those who heard him proved to us that it is true' (2:3). Some scholars have drawn inferences from this about the possible date of the book. But this statement does not necessarily imply that the writer belonged to a different generation from the apostles – only that he was not among their number. A person like Stephen would fit this description just as easily as a much later character.

● The author was clearly well-educated. He knew how to write Greek, and he was well versed in the literary and rhetorical conventions of the Hellenistic age. He also seems to have had some acquaintance with ideas that

The book of Hebrews was concerned to explain how Jesus related to the story of the Old Testament. Here a Jewish family celebrates the Feast of Tabernacles, or Booths – a reminder of the time Israel spent in tents in the desert after the exodus from Egypt.

were common among Greek thinkers. The way he contrasts the heavenly world, where Christ is, and the material world in which the Jewish ritual system exists, is not all that different from Plato's notion about the world of forms, or ideas, that gives meaning to the world we know through our senses.

● At the same time, the author's real background seems to be in Judaism. It has been argued that his knowledge of Plato's system came not through direct acquaintance with Greek thinking, but through knowledge of the work of a Hellenistic Jewish philosopher like Philo, who flourished in the early years of the Christian era at Alexandria in Egypt. But he also seems to have been familiar with the way the Jewish teachers in Palestine interpreted the Old Testament. In addition to that, some of his most distinctive imagery was very popular in various groups on the fringes of Judaism. The people from Qumran, who wrote the Dead Sea Scrolls, were expecting a Messiah who, like Jesus in Hebrews, would also be a high priest. They also had considerable interest in the Old Testament figure of Melchizedek and, like the writer of Hebrews, had a particular fascination with the rituals of the Day of Atonement. This has led some scholars to suggest that Hebrews was written to Christians who had come under the influence of the commune at Qumran. But some of these ideas are found in other Jewish documents like the *Testaments of the Twelve Patriarchs*, while purification ceremonies such as those mentioned in Hebrews 6:2 were observed by many groups in the Jewish community.

The readers

Since we cannot identify the author of Hebrews, we cannot expect to be certain who its first readers were. But there are a number of indications in the book itself that can help us to gain quite an accurate impression of the kind of people they were.

● Most modern readers have concluded that they were Jewish Christians. This is implied in the title, 'To the Hebrews'. But the author himself did not give the book this title: it was added for convenience in later centuries (like all the titles of our New Testament books). It could therefore be misleading. Some prefer to think of Gentile Christians as its recipients. But it is not easy to see why non-Jewish Christians should have had such a detailed interest in the sacrificial system of ancient Israel. Jewish Christians, of

course, would want to know what they were to make of it all, for to them the Old Testament and its rituals had been given by God. What was its status now? Had God somehow changed his mind with the coming of Jesus? These questions would certainly have more point for Jewish Christians than for Gentiles. They would be of greatest interest for Jewish Christians living in Jerusalem itself, and some have suggested that this is where Hebrews originated. But a number of facts speak against this:

i. The church at Jerusalem was always a poor church, whereas the readers of Hebrews seem to have been reasonably well off (6:10, 10:34).

ii. The temple is not actually mentioned in Hebrews. Instead, the author describes in great detail the worship associated with the tent of worship used by Moses and the Israelites in their desert journey from Egypt to Canaan. This suggests that his readers did not have firsthand experience of the temple, and their only direct access to rituals like sacrifice and priesthood was through what they could read for themselves in the books of Leviticus and Numbers. This would obviously suit the situation of Hellenist Jewish Christians living elsewhere in the Roman Empire.

● The readers of Hebrews also seem to have been involved in persecution. Not long after they became Christians, they had 'suffered many things, yet were not defeated by the struggle. You were at times publicly insulted and ill-treated, and at other times you were ready to join those who were being treated in this way. You shared the sufferings of prisoners, and when all your belongings were seized, you endured your loss gladly' (10:32-34). But the author then goes on to encourage his readers not to evade further persecution. Up to the time of writing, they had 'not yet had to resist to the point of being killed' (12:4), like some of the early Jerusalem Christians, but they should not shrink even from that.

● The book of Hebrews gives the impression that it is not addressed to an entire church, but to a group within a church. In 5:12-14 they are criticized because they have not yet realized their God-given potential to be teachers – a function that not every Christian would expect to have. Then 10:25 could be taken to suggest that they were reluctant to meet with other Christians – while 13:24 asks them to convey 'greetings to all your leaders and to all God's people'. It has been suggested that Hebrews may have been addressed to some sectarian

group mentioned elsewhere in the New Testament – perhaps the Colossian heretics, who were opposed by Paul in his letter to the church at Colossae. These people were certainly interested in the role of angels, and in some aspects of Jewish ritual practices. But they had no Jewish convictions. They saw the Old Testament rules as a useful way to achieve quite different objectives, and that would seem to distinguish them from the concerns of Hebrews.

● The recipients of Hebrews lived in Italy, perhaps in Rome. This is made clear in 13:24: 'The believers from Italy send you their greetings'. Whoever the author was, he was in the company of a group of Italian Christians who wished to be remembered by their friends at home. If this was in fact in Rome, the circumstances of the church there have some interesting similarities to the situation envisaged in Hebrews. The last chapter of Romans shows that in the late fifties the Roman church was not one unified congregation, but a collection of separate, though not unrelated 'house churches' (Romans 16:3-15). Other evidence from the Jewish community in Rome suggests that as the Christian gospel was proclaimed in different synagogues, they made different responses to it and formed Christian congregations distinguished by their various viewpoints on questions connected with Jewish observances. We also know that the Jews of Rome had a close interest in the kind of ideas that Hebrews shares with some fringe sects within Judaism.

The date

So when was Hebrews written? Various dates have been suggested, ranging from the early sixties to the end of the first century. On no account can it have been written later than about AD 90, for it is referred to in 1 Clement, which was written in Rome no later than AD 96. A number of arguments are involved in fixing a more precise date:

● Some have pointed to the statement in 2:3 that 'The Lord himself first announced this salvation, and those who heard him proved to us that it is true'. They argue that this shows the author was a second- or third-generation Christian, and would date Hebrews between AD 80 and 90. But we have already seen that this is not a necessary inference from that verse.

● It has also been pointed out that the book seems to emphasize the human character of Jesus, perhaps because this was the subject of controversy. This in turn would take us to the arguments about Jesus' humanity and divinity ('Docetism') that emerged towards the end of the first century. But when we examine such references closely, many of them are seen to be based on the outline of Jesus' life that we find in the Gospels, and they are used in Hebrews to provoke a specific recollection of Jesus' behaviour and actions as an example and encouragement (2:14; 4:15; 5:7-9; 13:12). If we compare this with the way 1 John opposes heresy (see chapter four below), we will find significant differences.

● In fact there are few signs of the interests of the institutional church in Hebrews. The tension between present experience (1:2; 6:5) and future hope (9:28; 10:34-38) that was so characteristic of the age of the apostles is still found – and there is no more church hierarchy in view than may be suggested by the vague title 'leaders' (13:24).

● The writer of Hebrews seems to suppose that the kind of worship described in the Old Testament was still in existence. 'The same sacrifices are offered for ever, year after year . . . the sacrifices serve year after year to remind people of their sins . . .' (10:1-3). These, and other similar statements, suggest that the temple in Jerusalem was still standing, and if that is the case then the book can be dated before AD 70. It may be objected that Hebrews refers not to the temple, but to the tent of worship in the desert. But the Old Testament regulations are the same in each case, and may indeed have the same origin if modern Old Testament scholars are to be believed. In fact there are no temple regulations as such in the Old Testament. Solomon's temple is just assumed to have taken over the pattern of worship already laid down in the Torah. If the temple had ceased to function when Hebrews was written, it is impossible to believe that the author would not have mentioned the fact, for the literal destruction of the Old Testament ritual in AD 70 was the final confirmation of the whole argument of his book.

● If Hebrews was directed to readers in Rome, then the statement that they had not yet given their lives for the gospel would seem to point to a time before Nero's persecution came to a climax in AD 64. The earlier persecution that they had suffered could then have been connected with the disturbances that led Claudius to expel the Jewish community from Rome for a time in AD 48.

Origins We may tentatively conclude that Hebrews was written by an unknown author in the period leading up to Nero's persecution. Its first readers were a group of Hellenist Jewish Christians in Rome who were trying to escape the consequences of being known as Christians by lapsing back into the practices of Judaism. They wanted the protection that the empire gave to Jews. But they also wished to enjoy the privileges of being Christians. The author of Hebrews deplored such a selfish attitude. They were betraying their fellow-Christians, and their acquiescence in Jewish rituals was in effect a denial of what Jesus had done for them. If they truly wished to serve him, they must be prepared to stand up and be counted as his followers, whatever the cost might be.

Hebrews and the Old Testament

The most distinctive feature of the book of Hebrews is the way that it uses the Old Testament to back up its arguments. Taking up Old Testament figures like Aaron or Melchizedek, and Old Testament rituals like the Day of Atonement, the author suggests that these things were a kind of symbolic preview of the work of Jesus. Just as Aaron was a high priest, so is Jesus – though with significantly greater effect. His position is more directly comparable to that of Melchizedek, and the sacrifice he offers has more lasting benefits than the Old Testament ritual of the Day of Atonement.

If we ever think about the Old Testament at all today, this is not the way we generally approach it. We may ask questions about its morality or its picture of God, but we would not expect to find detailed descriptions of the person of Jesus hidden within its pages. Yet our modern concerns are basically the same as those that concerned the author of Hebrews: namely, in what sense is the Old Testament a 'Christian' book? It was not written by Christians, of course, but the author of Hebrews shared the conviction of the early church (and of later Christians) that the God of whom the Old Testament speaks is the same God as Jesus revealed. Since God is unchangeable, it is therefore legitimate to look for some sort of unity between the Old Testament and the New Testament.

The author of Hebrews found this unity by supposing that, since the same God is involved in both parts of our Bible, his activities in the earlier stages of its story can be taken as a kind of pattern or visual aid for his activity in the later stages. It is in this light that we can understand the way the writer uses the Old Testament. He is not suggesting that the people of Old Testament times understood their history and priestly ritual as a kind of glimpse into the unknown future. To them, these things were the facts of everyday life. But when Christians looked back with the benefit of hindsight, they could see how the life, death and resurrection of Jesus could appropriately be described as the fulfilment of the Old Testament. Peter, for example, described Jesus as 'the Servant of God' (Acts 3:13, 26; 4:25-30), no doubt referring to those passages in the book of Isaiah that we call 'the Servant Songs' (Isaiah 42:1-4; 49:1-6; 50:4-9; 52:13–53:12). For Isaiah and his contemporaries, the Servant was a real person or persons – the whole nation of Israel, or perhaps the prophet himself. But as Peter looked back, he saw that these passages summed up Jesus' ministry in a special way. Hebrews is doing the same thing with other Old Testament people (Moses, Joshua, Aaron, Melchizedek) and things (the Day of Atonement and the rituals of the tent of worship in the desert).

This interpretation of the Old Testament was not unknown in Judaism. Philo of Alexandria had elevated it to an art, arguing that the apparently 'historical' events of the Old Testament were a kind of symbol of Greek philosophy, at least as he understood it from his own Jewish background. Many of the Church Fathers later read not only the Old Testament but also the New Testament in this way, ignoring the reality of its stories and regarding them instead as complex symbols of theological truths. This is how the fourth-century writer Hilary of Poitiers described the reasoning behind this: 'Every work contained in the sacred volume announces by word, explains by facts, and corroborates by examples the coming of our Lord Jesus Christ . . . From the beginning of the world Christ, by authentic and absolute prefigurations in the person of the Patriarchs, gives birth to the Church, washes it clean, sanctifies it, chooses it, places it apart and redeems it: by the sleep of Adam, by the deluge in the days of Noah, by the blessing of Melchizedek, by Abraham's justification, by the birth of Isaac, by the captivity of Jacob . . . The purpose of this work, is to show that in each personage, in every age, and in every act, the image of his coming, of his teaching, of his resurrection, and of our church is reflected as in a mirror.'

But Hebrews is not like that. It takes the Old Testament story seriously, and does not ignore its historical reality. It does not treat the Old Testament like an ancient *Pilgrim's Progress*. It is not a story with no meaning apart from what it may be held to symbolize. On the contrary, it records the actions of God in real history – and, in an important sense, when Hebrews compares Old and New Testaments, it concentrates not so much on their specific details as on the person of God himself. It is at pains to emphasize that what God has done in Jesus is continuous with – indeed grows out of – his revelation in the Old Testament.

Scholars have traditionally called this method of interpretation 'typology'. But this tells us little, for the same term is also used to describe the work of Philo and the Church Fathers, and Hebrews is certainly different from them. Hebrews draws attention to correspondences between Old and New Testaments, showing how God's work in one period of time was fulfilled and superseded by God's work in Jesus.

This method of expounding the Christian message is not found in any comprehensive form anywhere else in the New Testament. Its main appeal would obviously be to Christians with Jewish connections. It is far removed from the questions that modern Christians ask about the Old Testament, but its essential message is not irrelevant, for it is a reminder of the faithfulness and consistency of God's dealings with men and women at all times and in all places (Hebrews 13:8).

Christians and the Old Testament covenant

Genesis 12:1-3; 15; 17; 22:16-18;
Exodus 19:5-8; 20-24

The debates in the early church about Jewish morality and ritual were the symptoms of a much more fundamental problem. In Old Testament times, to be a member of the people of God was not simply a matter of behaving in the same way as other like-minded people. It also involved inclusion in the covenant relationship that God had established with Israel's ancestor Abraham, and with Moses at Mt Sinai. This relationship had started with God's concern and care for his people. Abraham was called from Mesopotamia and given a new homeland not because of any moral or spiritual superiority that he may have possessed, but simply because

It was on Mt Sinai that God gave Moses the Ten Commandments and other laws for the Israelites.

God's affection was centred on him. His descendants later emerged from the shattering experience of the exodus not because of their own moral perfection but simply through the care of a loving God.

On the basis of these undeserved acts of kindness, God had made certain demands of his people. Abraham and his family were promised a great and prosperous future. In response to God's goodness, Abraham had accepted that both he and his descendants should give tangible and lasting expression to this new covenant relationship that existed between them and God: 'You and your descendants must all agree to circumcise every male among you . . . This will show that there is a covenant between you and me . . . Any male who has not been circumcised will no longer be considered one of my people, because he has not kept the covenant with me.'

We find the same elements in the covenant relationship established between God and Israel through Moses at Mt Sinai. God had rescued his people from slavery in Egypt, and they were to respond with obedience to his laws – moral laws like the Ten Commandments, and also the ritual regulations that we find in Leviticus and Numbers.

When Christians claimed that Jesus had come to fulfil what God had promised in the Old Testament, these were the promises the Jewish people would inevitably recall. And the Christians themselves believed that what they were experiencing through the presence of Jesus and the power of the Holy Spirit made them the heirs of Abraham himself. This is why the Old Testament Law and circumcision became such important issues in the church. For on a plain reading of the Old Testament, this was the only way that a person (whether born as a Jew or a Gentile) could ever be a part of God's covenant people. At the very beginning, all Christians paid due attention to this, for they were all followers of the Jewish religion. But when Paul and others accepted into the church Gentiles who had not been circumcised and saw no reason for keeping the Old Testament Law, the basic theological argument between Jews and Christians was transformed into a burning practical issue. Traditional Jewish thinking suggested that people who would not obey the Torah could not expect God to work in their lives. But the activity of the Holy Spirit among these pagan Gentiles seemed to be no less spectacular than his work in the lives of those Christians who were also faithful Jews.

Paul was one of the first Christian preachers to be faced with this problem. He was quite sure that circumcision and keeping the Old Testament Law should not be required of Gentile Christians. But the Old Testament had made it perfectly clear that to share in the blessings promised by God a person must become a member of Abraham's family. Paul did not wish to deny that the Old Testament was the word of God – and his opponents were not slow to remind him that being a member of Abraham's family meant circumcision and obedience to the Law.

Paul tackled this problem in his letter to the Galatians. He argued that the blessings promised by God to Abraham did not

Genesis 15:1-6

Genesis 17:9-14

Exodus 19:4-8; 20; Leviticus; Numbers

Acts 10:44-48

come to fruition because he kept the Law. That did not even exist in his day. But, Paul argued, the relationship that Abraham enjoyed with God was a matter of faith. 'Abraham believed and was blessed, so all who believe are blessed as he was.' Circumcision was just an external sign to confirm that a person was trying to keep the Old Testament Law. But if the Law was now redundant, then circumcision had also lost its value. What should matter to the Christian is 'faith that works through love'. Paul's argument is explained in greater detail in the companion book to this, *Paul* (pages 51-54). The question is important to us here because we can trace the same issues in Peter's first letter.

Galatians 3:17

Galatians 3:9

Galatians 5:2-12
Galatians 5:6

1 Peter

Many of the same themes are found here, though in a different form. Abraham is mentioned only in passing, and in a different context altogether – and there is no sign of the complex theological arguments that Paul brings forward in Galatians and Romans. But Peter conveys the clear conviction that Gentile Christians are now the true successors to the people of God in Old Testament times. It also asserts that they have achieved this position as a result of their response in faith to what God has done for them. Like the family of Abraham, Christians owe their knowledge of God not to their own piety or insight, but to God's gracious action in showing his love for them. In the case of Israel, this had been demonstrated particularly in the exodus. For the Christian, 'it was the costly sacrifice of Christ, who was like a lamb without defect or flaw'.

1 Peter 3:6

1 Peter 2:9-10

1 Peter 1:19

The relationship of Christians to the Jewish covenants is the main subject of Paul's letter to the Galatians. 1 Peter was not written in the same controversial context. But that only makes more striking its emphasis on the fact that Christians are now the true 'family of Abraham' without compulsory obedience to the Old Testament Law. For it shows how this issue was soon settled in the church along the lines that Paul suggested.

● *The Christian's status.* These themes appear in the very first verse, where we are told that the letter is written 'To God's chosen people in the Dispersion throughout the provinces of Pontus, Galatia, Cappadocia, Asia, and Bithynia'. This opening is similar to the book of James. We noticed there that 'God's people in the Dispersion' could indicate Jewish people. But it is more likely to refer to the church. In the case of 1 Peter, there can be no doubt at all that Gentile Christian readers are in view.

1 Peter 1:1-12

1 Peter 1:14, 18; 2:9-10; 4:3

This initial greeting is followed by a thanksgiving to God, but this soon turns to an exhortation. Peter's readers are encouraged to praise God for his goodness to them, 'even though for a little while you may have to suffer various trials'. He tells them that such trials are insignificant when set against God's power. Christians already know something of this in the new life that they enjoy through Jesus. They can also look forward to 'the Day when Jesus Christ is revealed', when they will meet him face to face. Simple Gentile believers may find this difficult to understand – even the angels cannot fully do so – but what is happening to them now, and the

1 Peter 1:6

1 Peter 1:7

destiny that is waiting for them in the future, is all a part of God's plan that was first revealed in the Old Testament.

1 Peter 1:13–2:10

● *Christian development.* The writer then goes on to remind his readers that acceptance of the good news about Jesus imposes responsibilities as well as bestowing privileges. They must never forget that they are called to share their faith with others, both in word and in deed. Christ's death and resurrection has 'set you free

1 Peter 1:18

from the worthless manner of life handed down by your ancestors',

Peter uses the word-picture of 'living stones' to describe how Christians are built together into the fabric of a 'living temple' which rests on the foundation of the work of Jesus Christ.

and the recollection of all that this means should lead Christians to obey God, and share his love with their fellow-citizens.

They should also grow and develop in their Christian experience, being as eager for spiritual nourishment as a baby is for its mother's milk. This is how they will grow as Christians, so they can 'Come as living stones, and let yourselves be used in building the spiritual temple, where you will serve as holy priests to offer spiritual and

1 Peter 2:5-9

acceptable sacrifices to God through Jesus Christ'. As Christians mature in this way, they will demonstrate how they are 'the chosen race, the King's priests, the holy nation, God's own people'.

There is not another passage of comparable length in the whole New Testament where more Old Testament imagery that was originally applied to Abraham and his descendants is taken over and applied to the Christian church, the 'new Israel'. But there are also some interesting connections here with Paul's thinking. The picture of the church as a building constructed out of living stones (one of which, the 'cornerstone', is Jesus himself) is not dissimilar to Paul's description of the church as a living body made up of many parts, 'Christ's body'. Indeed, Paul may well have thought in the same terms himself, for in Romans he writes of Christians offering 'a living sacrifice' that will bring glory to God. So, when Peter says that all Christians are 'priests', he is saying the same thing as Paul when he declares that all Christians have a God-given ability that they must share with the church at large. But they use entirely different language from each other.

1 Corinthians 12:12-31

Romans 12:1-2

1 Peter 2:11–4:19
● *Christian behaviour.* Peter goes on to remind his readers that, as God's people, they have different standards from non-Christians. They are as much at home in pagan society as 'strangers and refugees'. Their only true allegiance is to God himself and so everything they do should be intended to glorify him alone. Even when they have to 'endure the pain of undeserved suffering', they can look to the example of Jesus. For 'when he was insulted, he did not answer back with an insult; when he suffered, he did not threaten, but placed his hopes in God, the righteous Judge'.

1 Peter 2:11

1 Peter 2:19

1 Peter 2:23

Exactly the same principles should determine how the Christian behaves at home. Christian wives should be ready to share the love of Christ with their husbands – and they for their part must treat their wives with respect and understanding. In a word, every believer should follow the advice of Jesus: 'love one another . . . and be kind and humble with one another. Do not pay back evil with evil or cursing with cursing; instead, pay back with a blessing.'

1 Peter 3:8-9

Peter knew that it is never easy to behave like this, especially when Christians are suffering unjust persecution. It involves putting God first so that a Christian's life is controlled not by whims and fancies, but by God himself. But it is always worthwhile in the end. 'The end of all things is near', and God's people should be especially careful how they behave. Suffering is just a temporary thing, and Christians must look beyond it to the judgement of God. They can trust themselves to his care, for he 'always keeps his promise'.

1 Peter 4:7

1 Peter 4:19

1 Peter 5:1-14
● *Serving Christ.* Finally, Peter gives advice to those who are, like himself, 'elders' or 'shepherds' in the church. They must not be domineering in any way, but should be 'examples to the flock', recognizing that the church will flourish only when all its members have 'put on the apron of humility' to serve one another. They would not be the first to do that, for Jesus himself had worn the apron of a slave in order to wash his disciples' feet. But above all, they must not lose their trust in God in the midst of persecution.

1 Peter 5:3

1 Peter 5:5

John 13:1-17

Even this is a part of God's plan for his covenant people: 'after you have suffered for a little while, the God of all grace, who calls you to share his eternal glory in union with Christ, will himself perfect you and give you firmness, strength, and a sure foundation.'

1 Peter 5:10

Who wrote 1 Peter?

1 Peter was well-known and widely read in the church from quite early times. 1 Clement refers to it (AD 96), as also does Polycarp (AD 70–155), while Irenaeus stated towards the end of the second century that it was written by the apostle Peter himself. There are good reasons to accept this view of its authorship:

● Much of its teaching is exactly what we would expect from a disciple of Jesus. Many aspects seem to echo the teaching of Jesus himself, sometimes following it quite closely.

The author seems to contrast the readers' knowledge of Jesus, which was second-hand, with his own firsthand knowledge, and he seems to have witnessed both the trials (2:21-24) and the crucifixion of Jesus (5:1). Some scholars also believe that certain passages contain allusions to Gospel stories in which Peter was particularly involved. Others have claimed that if this letter was the work of Peter, then we would expect to read much more about Jesus. But this argument depends on the mistaken assumption that an author must write everything he knows in everything he writes. We should also remember that Peter's reminiscences of the life and teaching of Jesus may well have been recorded in a comprehensive way already, in the Gospel of Mark.

● There are also a number of connections between 1 Peter and the speeches of Peter in the book of Acts. Jesus' cross is called 'the tree' in Peter's speech to the Jewish rulers (Acts 5:30) and in his sermon to Cornelius (10:39), and also in 1 Peter (2:24). In 1 Peter 2:22-24 Jesus is referred to in the language of the 'Servant Songs' of the book of Isaiah, and according to Acts, Peter consistently called Jesus 'the Servant of God' in his earliest preaching (Acts 3:13,26; 4:25-30). Jesus is also linked with the stone mentioned in Psalm 118:22 by Peter in his defence before the Jewish authorities, and again in 1 Peter 2:4 – and the emphasis on the fulfilment of Old Testament promises in Acts 3:18-24 is very similar to 1 Peter 1:10-12.

● There is no sign in 1 Peter of the

Similarities between the teaching of Jesus and Peter	
Christians should have an alert and watchful attitude	Luke 12:35 1 Peter 1:13
Christians have the privilege of calling God 'Father'	Luke 11:2 1 Peter 1:17
Christian conduct should cause non-believers to praise God	Matthew 5:16 1 Peter 2:12
Christians should not pay back evil for evil	Luke 6:28 1 Peter 3:9
There is joy to be had when the Christian is being persecuted for doing what God wants	Matthew 5:10 1 Peter 3:14
We will all have to give an account of ourselves to God on Judgement Day	Matthew 12:36 1 Peter 4:5
If Christians are insulted because they are followers of Jesus, they should be glad	Matthew 5:11 1 Peter 4:14
Christians should be characterized by humility, and God will make them great	Luke 14:11 1 Peter 5:6
Because God is caring for them, Christians should not be worried or anxious	Matthew 6:25-27 1 Peter 5:7

Peter encourages his readers not to give up their faith when times become hard, but to endure trials with patience, knowing that they are following Jesus' example and that they will receive God's blessing.

concerns and interests of the later institutional church. There is still a tension between what God has done in the life of his people already (1:8-9, 23) and what will be accomplished in the future with the return of Jesus himself (1:3-5, 7, 13; 4:13; 5:4). Nor is there any evidence of a developed hierarchy in church organization. The leaders of the church are simply 'elders' or 'shepherds' (5:1-4).

There are therefore good reasons for accepting the ancient view that Peter was the author of this letter. But a number of modern scholars have drawn attention to three other facts which may point in a different direction:

● Like Hebrews, 1 Peter is written in an exceptionally fine Greek literary style, and it is suggested that a Galilean fisherman would not be capable of this – especially one who was described as 'uneducated and common' (Acts 4:13). We have already seen that the Galilean origins of Peter, far from disqualifying him from knowing Greek, would actually point in the opposite direction. Nor can the statement in Acts mean that Peter was illiterate. The point is just the opposite, for the Jewish leaders were expressing their amazement at the *eloquence* of men who had come from the remote hillsides of Galilee. Some wish to associate Peter with the letter itself, but not with its written form, and they have suggested that since Silas acted as Peter's secretary (5:12), the Greek style really his and not Peter's.

● Why would Peter have written a letter to Gentile Christians living in Asia Minor when according to Galatians 2:8

he was 'an apostle to the Jews'? This question is often raised, but it is scarcely relevant. For one thing, Paul's statement was not intended as a hard and fast rule. Paul himself never kept it, for he preached the gospel to many Jews even though he described himself as 'apostle to the Gentiles'. In addition, we have already seen how Peter moved into the Gentile world at a relatively early date. Paul mentions Peter's extensive travels (1 Corinthians 9:5), and there is no good reason why he could not have visited some of the places to which this letter was sent. Many think that Paul himself was forbidden to go to this area precisely because Peter was already working there (Acts 16:6-10). On the other hand, we need to take seriously the statement about 'the messengers who announced the Good News' in 1 Peter 1:12, which seems to suggest that the writer of the letter had not been the one who first brought the Christian message to this area.

● It has also been argued that 1 Peter is too similar to Paul's letters to have been written by Peter. But this is hardly convincing. It presupposes that Paul was the odd man out in the early church, saying entirely different things from anyone else. We have already argued that this is an unrealistic way to look at Paul – and we also noted good reasons for believing that he and Peter saw eye to eye on most issues. So why should

1 Peter be entirely different from Paul's writings? In any case, the two are not identical. It is significant that though Peter's teaching on the church and the Old Testament covenants is so similar to Paul's, he uses altogether different language and imagery. The closest parallels between them are all in the ethical instructions. But these can be found in a similar form not only in Paul's writings, but elsewhere in the New Testament – and this suggests that both Paul and Peter were passing on moral advice that was widely accepted throughout the early church.

Date and origin

If Peter did indeed write this letter, then obviously we must date it before his death, which took place in the persecution of Christians begun by Nero in AD 64 or 65. But dating it more precisely than that depends on our interpretation of the various references to persecution that occur throughout the letter. We can make a number of observations about this:

● In all the organized persecutions of Christians that took place towards the end of the first century, obedience to the emperor – even worship of him – was a crucial test of Christian allegiance. But this was clearly *not* the case in the persecutions envisaged in 1 Peter. Christians are encouraged to 'respect

the Emperor', and to accept his authority – even though it must come second to the authority of God (2:13-17).

● The readers of 1 Peter seem to have been surprised to be persecuted (4:12) – and after the persecutions of Nero, we might have expected them to accept suffering as the norm.

● The descriptions of persecution in 5:8 ('Your enemy, the Devil, roams round like a roaring lion, looking for someone to devour') and 1:7 (testing by fire) could well refer to the events of Nero's persecution itself. According to the Roman historian Tacitus, the hated Christians 'were covered with wild beasts' skins and torn to death by dogs; or they were fastened on crosses, and, when daylight failed, were burned to serve as lamps by night' (*Annals* 15.44).

1 Peter 5:13

It may therefore be suggested that 1 Peter was written as the Neronic persecution of the Christians was in its early stages. We have no certain evidence that it eventually spread to Asia Minor. But even if it did not, the official persecution in Rome would certainly have encouraged people elsewhere to despise the Christians in their own cities. We do know that Peter was in Rome at the time. The term 'Babylon' was frequently used by the early Christians and others as a sort of code word for Rome. As Peter saw what was happening there, he felt that it would only be a matter of time before such a great evil must spread to other parts of the empire. He wanted his fellow-Christians to be assured that when the trial came, they were not alone in their suffering. Others were suffering too. But most important of all, God had them all in his care, for they were his covenant people.

Elders in the church should be like shepherds, says Peter: leaders who guide, tend and care for the people who are in their charge.

The theme of baptism in 1 Peter

On the surface, 1 Peter appears to be an ordinary letter, written to encourage Christians who were being persecuted. But some scholars have suggested that there is more to it than this. They have argued that the central part of 1 Peter (1:3–4:11) is not a letter at all, but an account of a service of baptism in the early church. They draw attention to a number of its features:

● This passage seems to be a self-contained section of the letter. The words of 4:11 would certainly make a suitable conclusion, for they contain a fuller benediction than we actually find at the end of chapter five. Peter also says in 5:12 that he is writing a 'brief letter', and since the whole of 1 Peter is hardly 'brief', the actual letter that he wrote may only run from 4:12 to 5:14, while the rest of the book is an account of the church's worship.

● Baptism is mentioned only in one obscure passage (3:18-22). This may be thought a good reason for doubting its importance. But in this passage, Noah's deliverance in the Old Testament is said to be 'a symbol pointing to baptism, which now saves you'. The emphasis on 'now' suggests to some that those addressed had only just been baptised. Others have claimed to be able to

discern subtle changes in the language towards the end of the first chapter, and they argue that the act of baptism had actually taken place between 1:21 and 1:22. On this understanding, this part of 1 Peter is regarded as a kind of account of the service of baptism, complete with hymns, responses, prayers, a sermon and a benediction. Other evidence for this is drawn from the exhortation to 'Be like new-born babies, always thirsty for the pure spiritual milk' (2:2). Evidence from the *Apostolic Tradition* ascribed to Hippolytus describes how towards the end of the second century a cup of milk and honey was given to Christians who had just been baptized, to remind them of the land promised to Israel ('a land flowing with milk and honey', Exodus 3:8). But 1 Peter mentions neither the honey nor the land, and the milk is described as 'pure and spiritual', which suggests it should be understood metaphorically rather than literally. Another link with the *Apostolic Tradition* has been found in 1 Peter 3:3. Here Christian women are reminded that a person's character has nothing to do with 'the way you do your hair, or the jewellery you put on, or the dresses you wear'. In later customs, women removed jewellery and clothing and rearranged

Baptism of both adult converts and children is practised today by Christians as a sign of their faith and a public expression of their intention to follow and serve Christ.

their hair before being baptized. But the emphasis in 1 Peter is not so much on this, as on the positive moral virtues that should be found in the Christian.

● There are a number of places where Peter uses language and imagery taken from the Passover story in the Old Testament. He says, for example, that Christ is 'a lamb without defect or flaw' (1:19), just as the Passover lambs had been (Exodus 12:5). Christians are told to 'gird up your minds' (1:13), in the same way as the Israelites fastened up their clothing on Passover night (Exodus 12:11). And 2:1-10 has many connections with the Old Testament books of Exodus, Leviticus and Numbers. The relevance of this Passover connection is found in the fact that Tertullian, writing at the end of the second century, says that the ideal time for Christians to be baptized was at Easter (Passover).

These arguments are very weak, and there is no compelling reason to think that 1 Peter contains an account of a service of baptism:

● We have no way of recognizing a first-century baptismal service, for we have no real idea how baptism was carried out in the earliest churches. Where the New Testament mentions it, baptism seems to have taken place at the same time as a person's initial commitment to Christianity. There is certainly no indication in the New Testament that baptism was an important event in the organized worship services of the church. No doubt Christians soon developed their own preferred ways of conducting worship. But it is highly unlikely that these were as stereotyped in the New Testament period as they were in the days of Hippolytus and Tertullian.

● It is also difficult to reconcile this theory with the plain evidence of 1 Peter. There is no indication at all that the section 1:3–4:11 has originated in a different context from the rest. It is written in exactly the same style, and the same arguments seem to carry over from one section to the other.

● This baptismal theory has no way of explaining how a baptismal liturgy for the church at Rome could have got mixed up with a letter to Christians in Asia Minor. On the face of it, 1 Peter is a letter to persecuted Christians, and we must make sense of it in that light.

The evidence that has been claimed in support of this theory could no doubt carry some weight if we had other reasons to connect 1 Peter with Christian baptism. But they are hardly sufficient in themselves to establish such a connection. In addition, there are important differences between the accounts of Hippolytus and what we read in 1 Peter. Later, the service of baptism included exorcism, anointing and the laying-on of hands – and there are no hints of any of these in 1 Peter.

The occurrence of themes that seem relevant to newly-baptized Christians is probably due to the fact that Peter, like Paul, wanted to remind his readers of what was involved in being a Christian. To do this, he needed to recall the commitment they had made when they first came to faith in Christ. Quite possibly he would repeat the sort of things that he was in the habit of saying to new converts. But that does not lead to the conclusion that he was giving an eyewitness report of an actual church service.

Once a preacher has worked out an effective way of expressing something, he will always tend to repeat the same ideas in different contexts. The author of this book has regularly expounded themes found in these pages in many a sermon – but that hardly justifies the conclusion that the whole book is some kind of worship manual for the services of the church!

Peter and the church in Rome

After the stories of the early chapters of Acts, the course of the rest of Peter's life is unknown to us. Apart from Paul's reference to his missionary activity (1 Corinthians 9:5), and what is perhaps a cryptic mention of his death in John 21:18-19, the New Testament tells us nothing more about him. 1 Peter, of course, is evidence that he was at one time in Rome – but it gives us no further personal details.

It was not long, however, before Christians began to enquire about Peter more specifically. Just as they wanted to know about Andrew, Matthew, Philip and other disciples of Jesus, so they wanted to know what had become of the disciple whom Jesus had once called 'the Rock', on whose foundation he said the church would be built (Matthew 16:17-19).

The second-century *Acts of Peter* purport to tell of how Peter came at an early stage to the city of Rome and there established a large and thriving Christian community. Like his Master before him, he performed many miracles, though his progress was continuously hindered by a pagan magician called Simon – who, among other things, had the power to fly. According to this document, Peter's mission to Rome was cut short by the events of Nero's persecution. His Christian friends advised him to leave the city and escape martyrdom. In that way he would be free for yet greater exploits in proclaiming the Christian message. But as he was leaving the city in disguise, Peter saw Jesus himself entering Rome. He asked Jesus where he was going (in Latin, *Quo vadis?*). 'And the Lord said to him, "I am coming to Rome to be crucified." . . . And Peter came to himself; . . . he returned to Rome rejoicing and giving praise to the Lord'. As a result of his return, Peter himself was crucified, insisting that he should be hung upside-down on the cross.

Like the stories about the other disciples, all this is mostly fiction. But, like them, it probably reflects some facts. For there is no reason to doubt either that Peter visited Rome and played an important part in the work of the church there, or that he was put to

death in the persecution started by Nero. 1 Clement 5 connects the deaths of both Peter and Paul with this period, and before the end of the second century the graves of these apostles were a place of pilgrimage (Eusebius, *Ecclesiastical History* 2.25.5-7). At a later date, when Constantine became a Christian, he erected a more elaborate shrine at the spot (probably in about AD 333), and today the Basilica of St Peter stands on the same site. All of this has been confirmed in recent investigations by archaeologists working beneath the Vatican. Not only has Constantine's monument been discovered, but traces of the second-century edifice have also been found. Further remains of bones and early graves, some going back to the first century, have also been discovered. But there is considerable disagreement among archaeologists about the significance of them. Some believe that the actual grave of Peter himself has been laid bare, while others argue that these graves are not even Christian. This is a genuine argument about the evidence: many Roman Catholic scholars do not believe that the grave of Peter is here, while some Protestants are quite convinced that it is. It is worth observing that the argument is unlikely to be resolved: even if we had the bones of Peter in front of us, no one could prove conclusively that they were his.

But we may be sure that Peter did die as a martyr in Rome during the persecution of Nero – and we can be reasonably certain that his grave lies somewhere on the site of St Peter's Basilica. But we have no evidence to show that he was the founder of the Roman church – though (along with Paul) he must have been the most important Christian leader to be connected with it, and it is therefore not surprising that he soon became its patron saint.

This 'graffiti wall' under St Peter's Basilica in Rome is said to contain the relics of the apostle Peter.

Hope for the future

Peter was not the first writer to face the problem of unjust suffering. It was a question that had come to be increasingly important to Jewish writers in the centuries just before the birth of Jesus.

The Old Testament had never understood God's relationship with men and women in exclusively personal and individual terms. Those who knew God best in ancient Israel found him not through isolated, mystical experiences, but in the events of everyday life. They believed that God was guiding and directing the history of their entire nation, and this meant that his people must express the meaning of their worship in the social institutions of national life. The Old Testament prophets went so far as to suggest that the whole course of Israel's history somehow depended on their

Isaiah 1:15-20; Jeremiah 8:4-12; Ezekiel 7:3-4

attitude to God. If the people were obedient to him, they prospered; if not, they could expect hard times.

These hard times had reached a climax when Jerusalem was captured by the Babylonian king Nebuchadnezzar in 586 BC. Not only did he invade the country, but he also took many of the people Jeremiah 52 to live in exile in Babylon. After only a short time there, the Jews had been allowed to return to their homeland – and those who Ezra, Nehemiah returned were determined not to repeat the mistakes of the past. They went out of their way to try and keep every detail of the Old Testament laws. But as things turned out, they did not prosper either. As time went on, the real way to prosperity seemed to lie more in collaboration with outsiders like the Romans than in remaining faithful to their own religion. Those who tried to keep the Old Testament faith alive found themselves more and more in a minority, and those who prospered often did so by sitting loosely to their fathers' faith, or even abandoning it altogether.

All this clearly demanded an explanation. Why did faithfulness not now lead to prosperity? Why were the faithful suffering? And why did God not put an end to the power of evil forces? Was there some contradiction between all this and the confident teaching of the Old Testament?

In the period from about 100 BC to AD 100, many Jewish writers put forward their own solution to these problems. Their books are so similar to one another that many modern scholars think of them as a distinct movement in Palestinian society. They have come to be known as 'apocalyptists' (people who reveal secret things), and the books they wrote are 'apocalypses', or revelations of secrets. These books have a number of distinctive features:

● They are almost always pessimistic about the world and its history. Unlike the Old Testament prophets, the apocalyptists despaired of God ever being able to work in the world. The forces of evil seemed too strong for that, and they saw the world running headlong to a final and tragic end. Since there was no point in trying to discover God at work in the midst of such apparent evil, the apocalyptic writers concentrated their attention on affairs in another, heavenly world. One of them stated that 'the Most High 2 Esdras 7:50 has made not one world but two', and many others shared his viewpoint. The apocalyptists believed that their job was to reveal events in God's world, and to assure their pious readers that, however much they may have been suffering, they still had a central place in God's plans.

● Their concern with the heavenly world led the apocalyptic writers to emphasize things like dreams, visions and communications by angels. If God was remote in his own world, he would naturally need to use go-betweens to communicate with people in our own world. So the typical apocalypse contains extensive reports of how its writer had received speculative visions and messages telling him what was going on in heaven.

● Along with this, they used a distinctive literary form. For apocalyptic visions were not described in straightforward terms.

Instead, they used a special kind of coded language. Mythological beasts and symbolic numbers feature prominently, usually accompanied by obscure quotations from other apocalyptic books.

● Apocalypses were also usually written under the name of some great figure from the past. Enoch, Noah, Adam, Moses, Ezra and various other Old Testament characters had apocalyptic works attributed to them. This may have been necessary because the Jews believed that the time of genuine prophecy had passed. But it is more likely that in times of persecution such authors wished to obscure their real identity for fear of reprisals.

On the face of it, this kind of escapism seems to be quite foreign to the outlook of the New Testament. But there is one New Testament book that has clearly been profoundly influenced by the style, if not the thinking, of the Jewish apocalyptists.

Revelation   Probably no book in the entire New Testament is less read and less understood than this one. All the great interpreters of the past had

The apocalyptic writings were full of strange and intricate symbolism, mysterious creatures and messages from angels. The German artist Albrecht Dürer captured the mood of these prophetic visions in his woodcut 'The Four Horsemen of the Apocalypse'.

difficulty with it. Martin Luther found it an offensive piece of work, with very little to say about Christ – and John Calvin also had grave doubts about its value. Many modern readers feel the same way, and see its message as a return to the worst of Jewish thinking, and by implication a denial of the message of Jesus himself.

It is not surprising that we should find Revelation a difficult book. We do not think in the same terms as Jewish apocalyptists. For us, their secret language and visions are both meaningless and bizarre. Many of us are uneasy with their conviction that God has no relevance to the world in which we live, and we find it difficult to imagine that his sole intention is to destroy human society and set up some sort of other-worldly kingdom instead. At the same time, there are others for whom the book of Revelation assumes far greater importance than many other books of the New Testament. They claim that it gives an insight into God's ultimate plans for humanity – even down to the details of how our present world will come to an end. So what can we make of it? Does it have any lasting significance, or is it to be dismissed as an unfortunate mistake by the early church, which should never have been included among the books of the New Testament?

A Christian book?

There can be no doubt that despair and pessimism about human history is fundamentally at odds with the outlook not only of the New Testament, but of the Old Testament as well. The biblical writers face up to the tragic realities of much of our human experience, but they have no doubt that God can and does meet men and women in the everyday events of normal life. God is not remote. How could he be, when through Jesus he has himself shared in our human existence? The writer of Hebrews, for instance, was quite sure that this was precisely why God can and does understand even the most trying aspects of life in this world.

Hebrews 4:14-16

When we look at the book of Revelation in detail, it is clear that its author shares this positive Christian emphasis on God's involvement in human affairs. Though the language and imagery in which he writes is apocalyptic in form, his message has a distinctive Christian emphasis.

● Unlike every other apocalyptic book, Revelation names both its author and its first readers. It was written by a person called John, and was sent 'From John to the seven churches in the province of Asia', in the towns of Ephesus, Smyrna, Pergamum, Thyatira, Sardis, Philadelphia and Laodicea. These churches are addressed in quite specific terms, and incidents and individuals are mentioned by name. This kind of self-confidence was never shared by the Jewish apocalyptic writers. On the contrary, they were generally so afraid of their persecutors that to have identified themselves in this way would have led to certain death. Of course, this is what it led to for some members of these churches. But that was no reason for disguising the true nature of their Christian faith.

Revelation 1:4

● Even in those parts of the book which are most similar to Jewish writings, John's visions are always closely linked to his

Revelation 1:10
Revelation 1:5-6; 12:10-12; 19:5-8;
22:13; 7:10, 12; 11:15, 17-18;
4:8, 11; 5:9-10; 15:3-4; 19:1-2

Isaiah 2:6-22; Hosea 2:14-23;
Joel 2:28–3:21

One of the letters to the seven
churches in Revelation was written to
Christians in Ephesus, the leading
city of the Roman province of Asia. In
Paul's day, Ephesus was a centre for
the worship of the goddess Diana
(Artemis), and later became known
for emperor-worship. The Temple of
Hadrian shown here dates from the
second century AD.

experience of life in the church. His vision comes to him 'on the Lord's day', perhaps in the course of Christian worship, and the contents of his visions have many references to the worship of the church: its confessions of faith, prayers and hymns.

● Revelation looks forward to a future intervention of God in the affairs of this world. But its understanding of this is different from that of the Jewish apocalyptists. Without exception, they regarded this world and all its affairs as irretrievably evil. History was a meaningless enigma, and the sooner its course was stopped, the better. This had not been the view of the Old Testament writers. Some of the prophets had looked forward to the coming of a 'Day of the Lord', when God would intervene in a final and decisive way in the affairs of the world. But they believed that this would be the continuation of what God was already doing in the present order of things: the God who would inaugurate a new world order in the future was also the God who could be known here and now in the events of human life.

The apocalyptic writers rejected this view, because they could make no sense of their own present experience. But like the Old Testament, the book of Revelation makes a clear link between what

God is doing in history now, and what he will do in the future. Indeed, the entire meaning of God's plan for the future of humanity is to be found in a historical event – the life, death and resurrection of Jesus himself, 'the Lamb of God'. And far from the sufferings of Christians being a meaningless interlude, John declares that it is one of the most powerful responses against all forms of evil.

Revelation 5

Revelation 12:10-12

Revelation therefore does not follow slavishly the pattern of the Jewish apocalyptic books. It presents a distinctive and positive

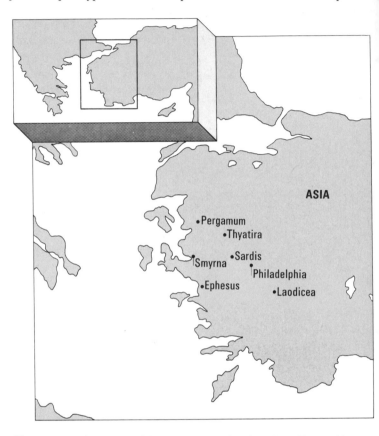

The seven churches of Revelation.

Christian explanation of the presence of evil in the affairs of human life. Its message is expressed through conventional Jewish language and vivid Old Testament imagery, but its content goes beyond the literary form of apocalyptic writing.

The book and its message

Revelation 1–3

The first three chapters of Revelation are similar to many other New Testament writings: they contain seven letters to seven churches in the Roman province of Asia. They are not real letters like those written by Paul, for they purport to come from the risen Jesus himself. John says that their content was given to him in a vision, just like the rest of the book. But they deal with very down-to-earth matters, and show a detailed knowledge of these people and their environment. Their churches were involved in disputes over Christian beliefs. Their commitment to Christ was wavering, and as a result they were in no position to face up to the challenge of state persecution. To do that, they needed to be whole-heartedly committed. This is a message that we find many times in the New Testament, and it is not significantly different from the message of 1 Peter.

Revelation 4—22

But the second part of the book is quite different. Here we come face to face with the language and imagery of apocalyptic writings. No longer do the visions seem to relate to real events and people. Instead, they introduce monsters and dragons in a quick succession of terrifying events. The whole section is introduced in chapters

Revelation 4—5

four and five by a vision of heaven. This sets the scene for what follows. Here the author sets out the basic way in which he understands God's workings in history. God is the one who is 'high

Isaiah 6:1; Revelation 4:2

and exalted' in absolute majesty and holiness. Men and women

Revelation 4:4

(represented by the twenty-four elders in the divine court) find their true significance as they worship and serve God. But they are quite incapable of reflecting every aspect of God's personality. When a sealed scroll is produced, containing God's revelation to the world, the elders are unable to open it to reveal its contents. After an angel has searched unsuccessfully in heaven, on earth and in the underworld, God's own heavenly deliverer appears on the scene –

Revelation 5:1-8

the Lamb of God, Jesus Christ.

This is a powerful and impressive presentation of the central importance of the life, death and resurrection of Jesus in the Christian understanding of life and its meaning. It is significant that at the very beginning of his visions, John links the future destiny of the world and its inhabitants with God's revelation of himself in the historical events of the life of Jesus.

The chapters that follow then present a series of visions describing how God judges all those forces that are implacably opposed to

Revelation 6:1—21:4

him. Many of the descriptions here are quite horrific, and much of the language in which God's judgement is described comes from the story of the plagues in Egypt in the Old Testament book of

Exodus 6:28—12:36

Exodus. This gives us a clue to the point that John is making. For in the exodus story, God's main purpose had not been the plagues. They were merely a prelude to the salvation that God had planned for his people – and through them, for the whole world. So too in Revelation, the main point of the book is not to be found in God's judgement upon evil, but in the conviction that God is now in the process of making a new world from which evil will be completely banished. In this new world, men and women will enjoy a new and unfettered freedom to know God in a direct way: 'God himself will be with them . . . He will wipe away all tears from their eyes. There will be no more death, no more grief or crying or pain. The old

Revelation 21:3-4

things have disappeared . . .'

There have been many attempts to arrange the visions of Revelation according to some sort of outline. One of the most attractive suggestions was first put forward by the German scholar Ernst Lohmeyer. He suggested that, with the exception of chapters

Revelation 21:5—22:21

four and five, and the description of the new heavens and earth, the whole book is arranged in a pattern of seven sections of sevens:

- Seven seals (6:1–8:1)
- Seven trumpets (8:2–11:19)
- Seven visions of the dragon and his kingdom (12:1–13:18)
- Seven visions of the Lamb of God and his coming (14:1-20)
- Seven bowls of God's anger against evil (15:1–16:21)
- Seven visions of the fall of 'Babylon' (17:1–19:10)
- Seven visions of the end (19:11–21:4)

What we have in these visions is a kaleidoscopic picture of how God will finally overcome the powers of evil. It is the work not of a self-conscious theologian but of a great artist, and like a good artist John depicts the same subject from a number of different perspectives, in order to reinforce the overall impression that he wants to create.

Making sense of the message

Revelation 2:10; 3:10

Revelation 18

It is difficult for us today to appreciate fully every detail of these visions. But we can readily understand their impact on the original readers of the book of Revelation. John assured his Christian readers that their present suffering was only temporary. Their great enemy 'Babylon' – a term which John, like Peter, used to refer to Rome – would ultimately come under the judgement of God. God would not allow injustice and evil to win the day, for he alone is the Lord of history. He has the destiny not only of nations, but of every one of his children in his personal control.

This view of Revelation is consistent with the way we have tried to appreciate the other New Testament books. It is sometimes called the 'Preterist' view of Revelation (from the Latin word *praeteritum*, 'referring to the past'), and it is a widely-held view.

But over the centuries, other readers of the New Testament fascinated by the seemingly mysterious character of Revelation's message, have refused to accept that its significance can be exhausted just by seeing what it meant for those Christians to whom it was first addressed. Some of the Church Fathers regarded it as a symbol of some of the great truths of the Christian faith. Origen and Augustine thought of its imagery as a symbolic account of the principles of God's working throughout history. They saw its weird descriptions of persons and battles and beasts not as real events, but as a dramatic presentation of the age-long opposition between God and the forces of evil. There is no doubt that this way of understanding Revelation can be very helpful. It makes sense of many of the most difficult passages in the book, and it also succeeds in relating it to the needs of its first readers – for they needed to be assured of the successful outcome of the struggle in which they were engaged.

But in the last 100 years or so, a large body of popular opinion has come to look at Revelation in a different way. The so-called 'futurists' argue that its real meaning is connected with events that are still in the future even now, and its full significance will become plain only to that generation which finds itself living in 'the last days'. Some have even suggested that the seven letters with which the book opens are not real letters at all, but part of a detailed clairvoyant insight given to John. They see them as detailed descriptions of seven successive ages of church history, reaching from the first century up to the end of time. Many of these so-called 'Dispensationalists' also believe that we today have reached the stage of the seventh and final letter (to Laodicea); so, they claim, our own generation is living at the very end of world history. There are many difficulties with views like this.

● There is of course the plain fact that several generations have believed themselves to be living in the last days – some even putting a date on the end of the world. But they have all been wrong.

● More serious is the fact that Jesus himself explicitly warned his disciples not to indulge in this kind of speculation: 'No one knows . . . when that day and hour will come – neither the angels in heaven, nor the Son; the Father alone knows.' If that is true, it is hardly likely that God would have given the information only to a select band of modern readers of the book of Revelation!

Matthew 24:36

● Another serious objection is that according to this view, the book of Revelation must have been totally meaningless and irrelevant to the people for whom it was ostensibly written. If the letters to the churches of Asia were not real letters, related to the concerns of real people, that would make Revelation quite different from every other book in the whole of the Bible. It also shares the general pessimism about existence in this world that we have seen to be the hallmark of Jewish apocalyptic literature – but something that is quite foreign to New Testament thinking. The God of the early church was not offering 'pie in the sky', but a living relationship with himself through Jesus Christ here and now in this present life.

There is no justification for regarding either Revelation or any other book of the Bible as a kind of blueprint for the future course of world events. That is not to suggest that the Christian faith has no expectation of a better world at some future date. The whole New Testament presents the clear conviction that there will be a point at which God must deal decisively with the forces of evil – and then, the new society of peace and justice announced by Jesus will become a lasting and tangible reality.

The book of Revelation confirms that conviction. It assures us that this world belongs to God and not to the forces of evil. It reminds us in vivid and powerful imagery that God will act to put things right, no matter how long his action may seem to be delayed. And when he acts, men and women will not simply be able to make a new start: they will have a part in the new world, where sin, misery and evil have no further place. Those who prefer to serve evil rather than God will have no part in the new world, just as Jesus himself had said. But God's intention is that no one should be excluded. The new living relationship established between God and humanity through the life, death and resurrection of Jesus is freely available to all those who will accept it, and the book of Revelation underlines that message: 'Come, whoever is thirsty: accept the water of life as a gift, whoever wants it.'

Revelation 21:27
Matthew 25:31-46

Revelation 22:17

The author and date of Revelation

The Roman emperor Domitian (AD 81–96).

Revelation is the only New Testament book that was dated by the Church Fathers. Irenaeus states that John saw his vision 'not long ago, but almost in our own generation, towards the end of Domitian's reign' (*Against Heresies* 5.30.3).

This corresponds quite closely with what we can see from the concerns of the book. Domitian (AD 81–96) demanded that all citizens should offer worship to him as a test of their political allegiance. Naturally, Christians did not want to be disloyal citizens – but they were not prepared to offer worship to the emperor. As a result, many of them were persecuted and hounded to death as enemies of the state.

A handful of scholars, however, do not accept this dating. Dr John Robinson, for example, argues that Revelation is to be set earlier, in the days just after the persecution of Christians by Nero. But Nero's persecution did not, so far as we know, involve the demand for emperor-worship. Robinson avoids this objection by suggesting that the author of Revelation had been in Rome during Nero's time, and saw worse to come. So he wrote his book to the Christians of Asia Minor not so much as an encouragement in the face of actual persecution, but as a warning of what they could expect soon. He also claims that careful analysis of the possible identities of the seven emperors listed in 17:9-11 leads to the time of Nero or his successor Galba (AD 68–69). But this (and other efforts to identify these characters) assumes that John had actual historical figures in mind at this point. It is just as likely that the seven emperors were not meant to be real people, but just the sum total of all the evil that is opposed to God.

On balance, there seems no compelling reason to reject the traditional date for Revelation of about AD 95.

The author of Revelation was a person called John. Justin Martyr states that this same John was 'one of the apostles of Christ' (*Dialogue with Trypho the Jew* 91). But many students of the New Testament find that hard to accept. The writer of Revelation seems to mention 'the twelve apostles of the Lamb' as a group that was quite separate from his own experience (21:14), and the way he writes of himself as 'your brother . . . a follower of Jesus . . . your partner' (1:9) hardly suggests he was a person of great authority in the church. But he was clearly steeped in the imagery of Jewish apocalyptic writings, and we may therefore suppose he was a Jew.

At the same time, there are a number of unusual connections between Revelation and the Gospel of John – and that document should almost certainly be linked with the apostle of that name. Both John and Revelation refer to Jesus as 'the word [*logos*] of God' (John 1:1-14; 1 John 1:1-4; Revelation 19:11-16). Both of them also call Jesus 'the Lamb of God', though they use different Greek words to do so (John 1:29; Revelation 5:6-14). Then we have the further fact that both the Gospel and the letters of John seem to have had some connection with the city of Ephesus – and that was one of the churches addressed in Revelation.

In view of all this, some have suggested that there was at Ephesus a 'school' of Christian thinkers established and inspired by John the apostle – and perhaps different members of this group, including John himself, were responsible for the final form of the various books which now go under his name.

4 The enemies within

THE MOST influential factor in the changing pattern of life in the early church was the emergence of various groups of people who came to be regarded as 'heretics' by the majority of Christian believers. But who were these people? We know a great deal about the heretical groups that prospered in the second century and later – Montanists, Gnostics, and others – but our information from the New Testament period is much less comprehensive. In the first century, the tensions that led to the eventual formation of separate sects were only just beginning to surface in church life, and the battle-lines that emerged towards the end of the second century were much more loosely drawn. Despite this, there are clear signs of moral and theological arguments in many of the New Testament books.

These arguments go back at least as far as the time of Paul. In his letter to the churches of Galatia, he wrote to counteract the influence of people whom he believed to be proclaiming 'another gospel'. Then, a few years later, in the church at Corinth he was again opposed by people with a fundamentally different under- standing of the Christian message. Probably none of these people were 'heretics' in the later, technical sense. Paul certainly never went so far as the second-century church leaders, by suggesting that they should be excluded from the church. Most of them seem to have been personal opponents of Paul, who sprang up spontaneously in a number of his churches, rather than the local representatives of any sort of organized group within the church at large.

Galatians 1:6

2 Corinthians 11:1-4

But it is clear that Paul was not wholly successful in despatching them altogether. For as we read some of the later New Testament books, we can see how the teachers opposed by Paul on a piecemeal basis were beginning to organize themselves into distinctive move- ments within the church.

The book of Revelation

We have already looked at the message of much of the book of Revelation. But in its first three chapters, this book reflects the conditions of the seven churches in Asia Minor to which it was addressed. The advice given by the risen Jesus to three of these churches (Ephesus, Pergamum and Thyatira) is about their attitude to various false teachers.

Revelation 2:1-7, 12-17, 18-29

The church at Ephesus is commended because it has 'tested those who say they are apostles but are not, and have found out that they are liars'. In addition, its members are said to 'hate what the Nicolaitans do'. In Pergamum, some church members had actually followed the teaching of these 'Nicolaitans'. Others were following 'the teaching of Balaam'. The church at Thyatira had also come under the influence of false teaching – in this case from 'that woman Jezebel, who calls herself a messenger of God'. According to John, this person was actually teaching about 'the deep secrets of Satan'.

Revelation 2:2, 6

Revelation 2:15, 14

Revelation 2:20

Revelation 2:24

There is some debate as to the precise identity of all these people. But they were probably all connected with each other, rather than being separate groups in different cities. The Nicolaitans are certainly mentioned in both Ephesus and Pergamum, and in the message to Pergamum the followers of Balaam appear to be the same people. Though neither of these names is applied to the heretics in Thyatira, the activities of the Nicolaitans/Balaamites in Pergamum are the same as those practised by 'Jezebel' and her devotees there: they all eat food offered to idols and indulge in immoral practices.

Paul had dealt with both these issues at an earlier period, though he never suggested that those involved in such activities were 'heretics' in the strict sense. Paul certainly denounced immorality, but he declared that eating food offered to idols was a matter of

The ruins of ancient Pergamum rise high above the modern Turkish town of Bergama. Pergamum was, according to Revelation, 'where Satan has his throne', possibly referring to the Altar of Zeus which was situated between the two trees, overlooking the town. Pergamum also became a centre of the official cult of emperor-worship.

128

1 Corinthians 8   indifference to Christian believers. Things must have changed in
the interim. In Paul's time, these things were mainly practical
issues – an understandable hangover from the pagan past of many
of his converts. But they had now become theological and doctrinal
issues. The book of Revelation gives no real indication of the kind
of beliefs that led to such activities. But a number of considerations
suggest that these sects were an early form of what was later known
as Gnosticism:

● One of the prominent Gnostic groups of the second century
actually called themselves 'Nicolaitans'. They traced their origins
back to a man called Nicolaus, who according to Acts was one of
Acts 6:5   Stephen's Hellenist colleagues in the early Jerusalem church. It is
unlikely that they had any real connection with this person. But
some of their practices were not dissimilar from what we read about
in the book of Revelation.

● Though the heretics opposed in Revelation were undoubtedly
less sophisticated and less well-organized than these later groups,
there are some signs of Gnostic terminology and ideas here. For
instance, Jezebel's teaching in Thyatira is referred to as 'the deep
Revelation 2:24   secrets of Satan', and this phrase is found among later Gnostic
groups as a description of their own beliefs. Then the very fact that
a woman should have been so prominent in this movement also
suggests a Gnostic type of thinking. For in the Gnostic heresies of
the second century, certain women played a large and conspicuous

The Gnostics laid great stress on mystical knowledge communicated to them alone. Members of the Aetherius Society, founded in 1954, listen to revelations from the skies. They claim that secret knowledge imparted to them by extra-terrestrial beings enables them to contribute to world peace and survival.

part. Indeed, this was one reason why the church after the New Testament period officially excluded women from any form of public service.

● The evidence of other New Testament books points in the same direction. The letters of John, as well as the letter of Jude and 2 Peter, all seem to have originated in the same area as Revelation, and in all of them we meet wandering teachers operating in the same way as those mentioned in Revelation. 1 John explains their theology in considerable detail, and we can see from that how clearly these heretics were moving towards classical Gnosticism.

Gnosticism

In describing the beliefs of some of the false teachers opposed in the New Testament writings, we have often noted their similarity with the second-century heresy, Gnosticism.

In reality, the Gnostics were not one, but many groups of heretics in the second and third centuries. Their thinking was based on the belief that there are two worlds: the world of spirit, where God is, which is holy and pure; and the world of matter, where we are, which is evil and corrupted. If God is holy and pure, they reasoned, then he can have nothing to do with our own world. Salvation therefore cannot be

relevant to this world, and the only hope is to escape to the spiritual world and find true fulfilment there.

For most Gnostics, this chance to escape came at death. But not everyone was qualified to reach the world of spirit. To do so, a person must have a divine 'spark' embedded in their nature, otherwise they would return to the world to start another meaningless round of material existence. Even those with the 'spark' could not be certain of finding ultimate release, for the evil creator of this world (the *Demiurge*) and his accomplices (the *Archons*) jealously guarded every passage to the world of

Part of the *Pistis Sophia*, a Gnostic manuscript which circulated in the late fourth or early fifth century.

spirit. The spark must be enlightened about its own nature and the nature of true salvation before it could hope to outwit them. For this it required 'knowledge' (*gnosis*). But when the Gnostic spoke of 'knowledge', it was not an intellectual knowledge of theology. It was a mystical experience, a direct 'knowing' of the supreme God.

It is not difficult to see why some of the false teachings we meet in the New Testament should be compared to all this. Paul's opponents in Corinth and Colossae, and the heretics opposed in the Pastoral Letters (1 and 2 Timothy, and Titus), Revelation, the letters of John, and Jude/2 Peter all laid great emphasis on such mystical 'knowledge' of God himself. They believed that through this they had already gained access to the world where God is, and so they had no further need of the traditional future hope of the church. Whatever Jesus may have been supposed to bring when he returned, they already possessed it – and so there was no need for him to come. They had already been released from the material ties of this world, and so they had no need of a future resurrection either.

In practical terms, this kind of belief could lead to two quite different extremes. Some argued that their aim of complete liberation from the forces of the material world could best be achieved by a rigorous asceticism which would effectively deny the reality of their bodily human existence. We can see traces of such beliefs in Paul's letter to the Colossians. The people whom Paul opposed there were trying to check 'the indulgence of the flesh' by the strict observance of all sorts of rules and regulations.

But there were others who were bolder than this. They had no doubt that they had already been released from all material ties, and so they believed that what they did in their present bodily existence was totally irrelevant to their ultimate spiritual destiny. They saw it as their duty to disregard everything connected with life in this world – including its standards of morality. So they indulged in the kind of undisciplined behaviour that is opposed by Paul in 1 Corinthians, and in Revelation, 1 John and Jude/2 Peter.

All of this is clearly reminiscent of second-century Gnosticism. But we need to remember that Gnosticism as a system did not exist in the first century, and the later Gnostic systems were far more complex than anything we find in the New Testament. The most we can say about the heretics mentioned there is that they seem to have held some ideas that later came to be incorporated into the major Gnostic systems. But they were not themselves Gnostics.

The letters of John

1 John 5:13
John 20:31

Like the Gospel of John, 1 John tells us why it was written. In chapter five, the writer says, 'I am writing this to you so that you may know that you have eternal life – you that believe in the Son of God'. The Gospel of John was written to demonstrate that Jesus was Messiah and Son of God – and to win people to faith in him. By contrast, 1 John was written to people who were already Christian believers. But they clearly needed to be reassured of the truth of what they believed.

The heretics

1 John 4:1

1 John 2:19

1 John 2:4; 4:8
1 John 4:1

1 John 1:6, 8, 10
1 John 1:5; 2:9
1 John 1:6, 8, 10; 2:4; 3:7-12; 4:20

It is not difficult to see why they needed such reassurance. Like the churches mentioned in Revelation, the church to which they belonged was suffering from the activities of 'false prophets'. These false prophets had originally been church members themselves. But they had left its fellowship, and they were now trying to subvert it from the outside. Of course, that was not how the false teachers saw things. They believed they had received special revelations that were not given to the ordinary church members. They spoke of 'knowing' God in an intimate way, through the special operation of the Holy Spirit in their lives. They also believed that this enabled them to live on a different plane from ordinary Christians. They were already spiritually 'perfect', living in full appreciation of the 'light' which was God himself – and so the normal earth-bound rules of Christian morality no longer applied to them.

All this sounds remarkably similar to the claims of Paul's opponents in Corinth. They too were claiming that because of their remarkable mystical experiences, they were no longer bound by the normal constraints of human existence. They believed that through these mystical experiences they had already been raised to a new spiritual level far above that enjoyed by ordinary Christians. It was, they said, just as if the resurrection had already come. They might seem to be living in this world, but really they had been totally liberated from it, and so they no longer shared its concerns.

People with similar views are also mentioned in Paul's second letter to Timothy. 1 John does not actually say that these false teachers also believed that the resurrection had already come in their own mystical experiences, but it is likely that they held this view too.

1 Corinthians 10:1-13

1 Corinthians 4:7-8

1 Corinthians 15:12-19

2 Timothy 2:17-18

In his first letter, John emphasizes that 'God is light and in him is no darkness at all'. His readers, surrounded by people advocating a pantheistic mysticism, needed reassuring of the clarity of God's truth.

Docetism

1 John 2:22-23; 4:2, 15; 5:1-5, 10-12

1 John 4:1-3

But there is a new element in 1 John. For the 'false prophets' mentioned here had a distinctive understanding of the person and significance of Jesus himself. It is clear from what he says that John's opponents were denying that Jesus was the Messiah and the Son of God. It was not that they denied that Jesus had revealed the power of God. But they found it difficult to see how an ordinary human person could reveal the character of the eternal God. So they asserted that Jesus was not truly human at all.

In Greek thinking there had always been a strong conviction that this world in which we live is quite separate from God's heavenly world. The Old Testament prophets had always believed that God's activity could be seen in the affairs of human experience. But Greek thinkers had regarded life in this world as a miserable existence. The true destiny of men and women, they claimed, was not here, but in the spiritual world inhabited by God. True salvation, therefore, could only consist in the escape of a person from the 'prison' of this world into the life of the supernatural world. There were many theories to explain precisely how this could be accomplished, and it is obvious that the desire for such liberation was what motivated both Paul's opponents in Corinth, and the false teachers of the church to which 1 John was addressed.

At the beginning, Christians were interested in such ideas mainly because they were attracted by the promise of exciting mystical experiences. But as these mystics began to think out the theological implications of their experience, they inevitably found it hard to cope with the church's belief that Jesus had come from God himself. For if God was a part of this mystical, supernatural world, then there was no way in which he could also be a real human person. For the all-powerful God to be imprisoned in the life of a human being would be a contradiction in terms.

One way out of the dilemma was to suggest that Jesus had only *seemed* to be the Messiah or Son of God. This view is called 'Docetism' (from the Greek word *dokeō*, 'to seem'), and this is the view that is opposed in 1 John. Many of the early Church Fathers mention people with such beliefs. Irenaeus tells how the apostle John once went to a public bath-house in Ephesus. But when he got there, John refused to take a bath because Cerinthus, who was himself a prominent Docetist, was also there.

Against Heresies 3.3.4

Some have suggested that 1 John was a direct reply to Cerinthus himself. He argued that the 'divine essence', or 'Christ', came into the human Jesus at his baptism, and left him before the crucifixion – and 1 John includes a statement that can be seen as a reply to this: 'Jesus Christ is the one who came with the water of his baptism and the blood of his death. He came not only with the water, but with both the water and the blood.' But Cerinthus had many other ideas not mentioned at all in 1 John, and the problems dealt with in this letter are undoubtedly less complex than the theology of Cerinthus and his followers. Indeed, with the exception of their speculation about the person of Christ, the heretics of 1 John have much more in common with Paul's opponents in

1 John 5:6

Corinth, and it is probably more accurate to regard them as an intermediate stage between the Corinthian heretics and the fully-developed Gnostic systems of the second century.

1 John   The author of 1 John clearly had no time for these people. He denounced their beliefs and opposed their practices in every section of his letter. He realized all too well the strong pressure that they were placing on the members of the church, and he went out of his way to assure them that they, and not the heretics, were the ones who had the truth.

But it is not easy to find any logical argument here. Some scholars have tried to rearrange John's letter to make it fit together more logically. Others have explained what they regard as inconsistencies by supposing that the letter went through more than one edition and is therefore the work of more than one writer. But none of these suggestions is particularly convincing. The book contains not just the author's response to the heretics. It is also a part of his own theological reflection on the situation which he faced, and for that reason it is more a work of art than a book of theology. It can usefully be compared to a musical composition, in which the main theme is first expounded, and then is taken up and developed and elaborated as the composer moves on to other themes and ideas yet always returning to his first thought.

The message   Whatever the form of the argument, the message of 1 John is crystal clear. Like every other New Testament writer, John is convinced that mystical experiences, however elevated, are totally irrelevant to Christian faith unless they affect the way people behave. It is no use talking about being liberated into the world of light, unless God's light truly informs and inspires our behaviour. To say that mystical experiences actually release men and women from the power of evil is unrealistic and untrue. Anyone who claims to be perfect and free

1 John 1   from the influence of sin is fooling himself.

True Christians must 'live just as Jesus Christ did' – but they must also accept the reality of their moral poverty, and accept the

1 John 2:1-6   forgiveness which only Jesus can give. Living like Jesus is a practical affair: it is a matter of loving other people, and this means that anyone who despises others (as did the Docetists) can hardly claim

1 John 2:7-16   to be doing God's will. In reality, they are just indulging their own
1 John 2:15-17   selfishness.

The fact that such people could ever have been a part of the church should serve to emphasize that the day of judgement is not

1 John 2:18-19   far off. The others must not be intimidated by them. Whatever the heretics may claim, those in the church are the true recipients of the

1 John 2:20-29   Holy Spirit, and they are the ones who have been accepted by God. Not that they have done anything to deserve that love. But having been adopted as God's children, they should ensure that they

1 John 3:1-10   continue to do as he wants. Just as Christ loved them, so they must
1 John 3:11-18   love one another – then they can be sure that they are truly living
1 John 3:19-24   in harmony with the Holy Spirit, and in union with God himself.

But telling the true from the false is not just a matter of human judgement. There is a test of belief that can distinguish the heretics from the true believers: 'anyone who acknowledges that Jesus Christ came as a human being has the Spirit who comes from God. But anyone who denies this about Jesus does not have the Spirit from God.' Having God's Spirit naturally leads to love, just as God himself is love. It also leads to obedience to God's commands, and to final victory over all that is opposed to his will. With this assurance, true Christians can be certain that they will know and understand God in a way that the Docetists never could.

1 John 4:1-6
1 John 4:7-21
1 John 5:1-5

1 John 5:6-21

The books by John

'Our love should not be just words and talk; it must be true love, which shows itself in action', wrote John. Relief supplies for Kampuchea, provided by an international Christian agency, are a demonstration of Christian concern to show the love of God in action.

We cannot consider 1 John independently from the other letters of John, and John's Gospel. 2 and 3 John are related very closely to 1 John, though they are quite different types of literature. Unlike 1 John, they are short, personal letters, one addressed to a church and the other to an individual called Gaius. Their author calls himself 'the Elder'. In 2 John he warns his readers against wandering teachers 'who do not acknowledge that Jesus Christ came as a human being' (2 John 7-11). He was concerned that these people should not be welcomed into the

church, and because of this many scholars think that 2 John must have been written before 1 John. For in 1 John the heretics had already been excluded from the church (1 John 2:19).

3 John advises Gaius about a man by the name of Diotrephes. He was aspiring to be the leader of the church, and 'the Elder' says that he intends to pay a short visit to correct 'the terrible things he says about us and the lies he tells' (3 John 9-10). Professor Ernst Käsemann has suggested that the way 'the Elder' writes here indicates that he himself was the heretic, and that it was

Diotrephes who was trying to preserve the integrity and faith of the church. But there is no evidence to support this view. The little that is said in 3 John does not suggest that there was any theological disagreement between 'the Elder' and Diotrephes – while 2 John (quite apart from John and 1 John) hardly suggests that its author held a Docetic theology.

It is more likely that 3 John reflects a stage when new patterns of church leadership were beginning to emerge. As the apostles and their representatives died, the corporate leadership of the earliest churches began to disappear, and new leaders were trying to assert themselves. This process eventually led to the formal appointment of just one authoritative leader in each local church. Perhaps 'the Elder' represented the older form of church organization, and that may explain his concern about the emergence of just one person claiming to be the church's leader. In the second century, anyone with the title of 'Elder' would himself have been a part of the organized hierarchy of the church. But the writer of these letters clearly does not belong in that context. He was obviously highly respected by his readers, but he does not seem to have

presuppose some knowledge of the issues dealt with in the first letter. So if we can decide the identity of 'the Elder', we can presumably identify the writer of all three letters.

But this is easier said than done. Scholars have often turned for guidance to a statement attributed to Papias. He was bishop of Hierapolis in the early second century, and wrote five books entitled *The Interpretation of the Oracles of the Lord*. Unfortunately, these are all now lost, and our only knowledge of them comes through a few scattered quotations in the works of Irenaeus and Eusebius. Eusebius quotes a statement in which Papias tells how he obtained his information about the earliest days of the church: 'if ever anyone came who had followed the elders, I inquired into the words of the elders, what Andrew or Peter or Philip or Thomas or James or John or Matthew, or any other of the Lord's disciples, had said, and what Aristion and the elder John, the Lord's disciples, were saying.' Eusebius goes on to observe that 'It is here worth noting that he twice counts the name of John, and reckons the first John with . . . the other Apostles . . . but places the second with the others outside the

Hierapolis was situated about 6 miles/10km north of Laodicea in the Lycus Valley in what is now Turkey. It was a centre of pagan cults and became important because of the healing powers of its hot springs, from which came pools and rock channels. There is a reference to their 'lukewarm' water in the letter to Laodicea in the book of Revelation.

had absolute authority over them. He can only appeal to them to do what he believed to be right.

The majority of scholars believe that 'the Elder' who wrote 2 and 3 John also wrote 1 John. There are many connections between the three letters in vocabulary and style, and certain statements in 2 and 3 John seem to

number of the apostles . . . This confirms the truth of the story of those who have said that there were two of the same name in Asia, and that there are two tombs at Ephesus both still called John's.' (Eusebius, *Ecclesiastical History* 3.39.4-6)

If the 'elder John' to whom Eusebius refers was the same person as 'the

Elder' who wrote 2 and 3 John, then presumably this second-generation Christian was also the author of 1 John (and perhaps of the Gospel of John). But some scholars have pointed out that Papias's statement is ambiguous, for he also appears to call the disciples themselves 'elders'. Eusebius may therefore be wrong to infer that Papias was referring to two different Johns.

Of course, this whole argument assumes that Papias had access to reliable information. But we must treat the statements of the Church Fathers with caution, especially when we only have second-hand knowledge of what Papias actually wrote. So far as the writings of John are concerned, it is more helpful to begin with the documents themselves.

There is a certain amount of debate about the precise relationship between 1, 2 and 3 John, and the Gospel of John. There are considerable and close similarities between the Gospel and 1 John. Both use the same language in the same way. The contrasts between light and darkness, life and death, truth and error, and the emphasis on love – not to mention the description of Jesus as the Word or *Logos* – are all found in both Gospel and letter. Both of them also use the same techniques for conveying their message, initially stating an idea in a simple and easily-remembered way, and then examining its implications from a number of different angles.

But there are also a number of differences. 1 John has a more restricted vocabulary than the Gospel. Its emphasis is also slightly different at some points. For instance, while the Gospel lays most emphasis on the present experience of the Christian (so-called 'realized eschatology'), the letter has much more emphasis on the future hope. The letter also has a stronger emphasis on the church and its sacraments – though here again, these things are not entirely absent from the Gospel.

Rudolf Bultmann suggested that the Gospel was edited by the writer of the letter, to bring it into line with his own thinking on these points. There is certainly some evidence that the Gospel contains the work of more than one person. But it is unlikely that the original form of the Gospel has been revised by someone who found it theologically unacceptable. An explanation of the complex connections between the various books connected with the name of John is the suggestion that there was in Ephesus a 'school' of Christian thinking associated with and growing out of the work of John, the disciple of Jesus. He served as the theological mentor of a whole group of Christians, and was the source of the information contained in the fourth Gospel (see John 21:24). But the literature as we know it now was the product of this 'school' rather than of just one individual.

In the book in this series *Jesus and the four Gospels*, I have suggested that the Gospel of John was first written in what we might call a 'Palestinian edition'. If so, then the Gospel would possibly be the first of these books to be edited and reissued from the school in Ephesus. Perhaps its message was subsequently misunderstood and misapplied by its new readers. In a Jewish context, the contrasts between darkness and light, truth and error, life and death were ethical contrasts. But the same terms had always been used by Greek thinkers to describe the cosmological distinction between the divine world of spirit, in which God lives, and the evil world of matter, where we live. Some Greek readers of the Gospel could easily have been misled by these terms – and that misunderstanding ultimately led them to the position adopted by the Docetists. The way the Gospel emphasizes the present reality of the resurrection in the life of Christian believers would also lend colour to such speculations.

In response to this growing threat, 'the Elder' (presumably a prominent member of the Johannine school – perhaps John himself) wrote 2 John to warn against such false teaching. But things went from bad to worse, the false teachers broke away from the church to form their own sect and 1 John was written as a more theological response to the problem. Not only was the Docetic view of Jesus challenged, but it was now emphasized that the resurrection hope was very much something tangible and future, and not just a part of the present spiritual experience of Christians.

If this reconstruction is correct, the date we give to these letters will depend on the date we give to the Gospel. The kind of teaching opposed in 1 John is certainly more advanced than that opposed by Paul in Corinth. There is a clear idea of 'heresy' in 1 John, but it is not as complex as we find in the second century. Nor does the relationship between 'the Elder' and his readers seem to be based on any kind of formal authority, such as we find in the second century. Since the heretics opposed in 1 John seem to have a number of features in common with those mentioned in Revelation, a date sometime towards the end of the first century is perhaps the nearest guess we can make.

Jude and 2 Peter

The influence of false teachers is also the subject of two of the most obscure books of the New Testament: Jude and 2 Peter. These books clearly belong together, for almost the whole of Jude (in a slightly modified form) is contained in 2 Peter. But otherwise, neither book contains any information to help us identify their original readers.

The heresy

The way in which Jude and 2 Peter oppose false teachers suggests that they originated in a situation quite similar to that dealt with in the opening chapters of the book of Revelation. The term 'gnosis' (knowledge) is not actually mentioned, but they are described as

Jude 19

'psychics' ('controlled by their natural desires'), and we know that this was a technical term used by the Gnostics. These people

Jude 8

certainly laid a great emphasis on their own spiritual experiences, and they argued that because they themselves had been 'raised' to a new level of spiritual life, they had also been released from the

Jude 12-13, 16, 18, 23

normal constraints of Christian morality. But all this was unacceptable to those in the mainstream of the church. Jude reminds them that even in Old Testament times God had punished people for the same kind of wrongdoing – and unless his readers were prepared to

Jude 8-16

repent, they could expect to share the same fate.

2 Peter 3:1-18

2 Peter also suggests that these people were denying the reality of the future coming of Jesus. No doubt they argued that since they themselves had already been spiritually 'raised' to heaven, there would be no further need for the kind of literal resurrection hope held by the majority of the early Christians. In any case, they said, nothing had happened, even though the church had fervently expected Jesus to return in glory. This argument had first been put

1 Corinthians 15:1-34

forward by Paul's opponents in Corinth. But 2 Peter introduces a new answer to it, by asserting that God's time-scale is not the same as ours: 'There is no difference in the Lord's sight between one day

2 Peter 3:8

and a thousand years . . .' The fact that the end has not yet arrived does not mean that God has failed to fulfil his promises. Quite the opposite is true, for the delay in the coming of Jesus is itself an expression of God's patience in allowing men and women more time to repent.

Jude does not describe the beliefs of these heretics so precisely. He simply asserts that they 'reject Jesus Christ, our only Master and

Jude 4

Lord'. It seems likely that these false teachers had not gone quite as far as those who were opposed in 1 John. They had not challenged the church's beliefs on a theological level, by declaring that Jesus was not the Son of God come in the flesh. Instead, like the heretics

Numbers 22:1-35; Jude 11; Revelation 2:14

mentioned in Revelation, they had 'given themselves over to the error that Balaam committed' – and, as we have already seen, that was more of a moral and practical problem.

Authors and dates

Neither Jude nor 2 Peter contains any information at all that might link them to specific events or people in the early church. The only way we can understand their background is by trying to fit them into what we know about the development of the early churches in general. A number of indications seem to suggest that both these books belong to the end of the New Testament period, rather than the time of the apostles themselves:

● Unlike Paul (and 1 John), Jude does not set out to argue with his opponents. He simply denounces them, and asserts that the answer to their problems is a return to 'the faith which once and for all God has given to his people' (Jude 3). We have seen in a previous chapter that the development of a standard form of belief like this was one of the things that characterized the emerging institutional church at the end of the first century.

● Jude 17 also indicates a date later than the age of the apostles, when the writer refers to 'what you were told in the past by the apostles of our Lord Jesus Christ'. Of course, that might refer to some occasion on which the readers had actually met the apostles themselves. But the same cannot be said of the reference to Paul in 2 Peter 3:14-16. Here, Paul's letters are mentioned as a recognized and well-known collection of writings, and they are also classed as 'scripture'. Paul's letters were probably not gathered together in a collection until after his death, and we can be sure that it would take a little longer again for them to be regarded as 'scripture' in any authoritative sense.

Most modern scholars interpret these facts to indicate that both these books must be dated sometime in the second century. Some would place them as late as AD 150. But there are difficulties about such a late date:

● It seems quite likely that 2 Peter was used (along with other New Testament books) by the unknown author of a work called *The Apocalypse of Peter*. But this is commonly dated sometime in the period between AD 100 and 135, and so 2 Peter can hardly be later than that.

● There is also the fact that the description of the false teachers in Jude and 2 Peter is quite different from any known second-century heresy. There is no hint even of a Docetic view of Jesus, let alone of the more complex theories of the classical Gnostic systems.

● There is also no trace of much of the apparatus of the second-century church. There is a consciousness of a fixed body of Christian doctrine, but there is no indication of an organized ministry in the church. Both Jude and 2 Peter appeal to their readers on a moral basis rather than on an authoritarian one.

A minority of scholars therefore have tried to explain the origin of these books by recourse to their opening sentences.

For both of them appear to be claiming to be the work of people who flourished in the age of the apostles themselves. 'Jude, servant of Jesus Christ, and brother of James' (Jude 1) is almost certainly meant to be that Jude who is named in the Gospels as a brother of Jesus and of James in Mark 6:3; while 'Simon Peter' is clearly intended to identify the author of 2 Peter as the apostle himself (2 Peter 1:1). But there are other problems involved here:

● The early church had a number of doubts about both these books. Jude is mentioned occasionally by the early Church Fathers, but 2 Peter is mentioned nowhere before the works of Origen (AD 185–254), and as late as the fourth century both of them were regarded either as spurious or of doubtful value. This at the very least must suggest that they were not generally supposed to be the writings of leaders of the first generation of Christians.

● Coupled with this, there is general agreement among scholars of all opinions that if 1 Peter is the work of Peter, the disciple of Jesus, then 2 Peter is not. Many writers in the early church were perplexed by the differences between the two, for in style of writing, theological emphasis and general

outlook they are so different that it is impossible to think the same person wrote them both. So if we are correct to connect 1 Peter with Peter himself, then we must look elsewhere for an explanation of 2 Peter.

An ingenious solution to this problem has recently been put forward by Dr John Robinson. He points out that the writer of Jude tells us that he was in the process of writing a letter to his readers, when he suddenly realized a more urgent need to communicate with them immediately – and in response to that, he wrote the letter of Jude (Jude 3). But what was the original letter that he was busy writing? In view of the close connections between them, could it have been 2 Peter? And could it be that the earlier letter that is referred to in 2 Peter 3:1 was not 1 Peter, as most people have thought, but Jude? Dr Robinson goes on to suggest that Jude may well have been writing as Peter's representative, and he points out that according to Acts 15:14,

the leaders of the Jewish church commonly referred to Peter as 'Simon', which could explain the unusual use of that name in the opening sentence of 2 Peter.

Of course, the problem with this is that we know nothing at all about the activities of the Jude who was the brother of James and of Jesus. But there is nevertheless a good deal to commend this suggestion. It is more difficult to go along with Dr Robinson and date the writing of both these books sometime between AD 60 and 62. If, as we have suggested, the heresy being opposed here is similar to that found in the seven churches of the book of Revelation, then we must look for a date nearer the end of the first century. The other pointers indicating a late date must also be taken seriously, and we know that the kind of practical immorality mentioned in Jude was much more common around AD 100 than it was in the middle of the first century.

Christians in Uganda know what it means to suffer for their faith; nevertheless, they are enthusiastic to share the good news about Jesus. Here, members of a mission team in Kigezi hold up copies of the Gospels before setting out on an evangelistic visit.

It may well be that Jude and 2 Peter both originate from a group of Peter's disciples, in much the same way as we suggested the Johannine letters originated from a 'school' of John's disciples. This could explain both the similarities and the differences between

2 Peter 1:16-18

Despite attack and opposition, persecution and heresy, the Christian church has shown an amazing ability to survive through the centuries. It often grows most vigorously when conditions seem at their bleakest.

Jude 24-25

ı and 2 Peter. It could also explain why certain sections of 2 Peter (like the description of the transfiguration of Jesus in chapter one) have struck many readers as authentic reminiscences of Peter himself. Perhaps what we have in both these short letters is a fresh application of the teaching of Peter to the concerns and interests of a Hellenistic Jewish Christian congregation somewhere in Asia Minor towards the end of the first century.

As the years passed, the church had to change and adapt itself to deal with new threats and take advantage of new opportunities. But it never forgot that its thinking and behaviour must always be firmly anchored in the experiences and outlook of those first followers who had actually known Jesus. Had it not been for the continuing commitment of a small group of Palestinian peasants, the wider world would never have heard this life-changing message. It was not easy for them. Their courage and boldness was rewarded with persecution, and even death. But their own experience of Jesus was such that they had no thought of turning back. They knew that Jesus was not dead, but alive – and working in power in their own lives through the presence of his Spirit. Not only did he inspire them to great exploits, but he also strengthened them in their trials. And it is no coincidence that one of the latest New Testament writings should sum up their deepest conviction in some of the most striking language of the entire Bible: 'To him who is able to keep you from falling, and to bring you faultless and joyful before his glorious presence – to the only God our Saviour, through Jesus Christ our Lord, be glory, majesty, might and authority, from all ages past, and now, and for ever and ever!'

Sources of quotations

The Bible: all quotations are from the
Good News Bible

Chapter One

T. W. Manson, 'The work of St. Luke',
in *Studies in the Gospels and Epistles*,
Lutterworth/Westminster Press, 1962,
pp. 46–67.
C. S. C. Williams, *A Commentary on the
Acts of the Apostles*, Black/Harper &
Row, 1964.

N. Perrin, *The New Testament. An
Introduction*. Harcourt, Brace
Jovanovich, 1974, p. 204.
Ph. Vielhauer, 'On the "Paulinism" of
Acts', in *Studies in Luke-Acts*, ed. L. E.
Keck & J. L. Martyn, Abingdon Press,
1966/SPCK, 1968, pp. 33–50.

Chapter Two

E. Haenchen, *The Acts of the Apostles*,
Blackwell, 1971.

Karl Kautsky, *The Foundations of
Christianity*, Allen & Unwin
Ltd/International Publishers, 1925.

E. Käsemann, *Essays on New Testament
Themes*, SCM Press, 1963/Allenson,
p. 81.

H. Berkhof, *Christian Faith*, Eerdmans,
1979/T. & T. Clark, 1980, p. 400.

Hans Küng, *On Being a Christian*,
Doubleday/Collins, 1977; *The Church*,
Burns & Oates, 1967/Sheed & Ward,
1968.

W. Bauer, *Orthodoxy and Heresy in
Earliest Christianity*, Fortress Press,
1971/SCM Press, 1972.

R. P. C. Hanson, *Christian Priesthood
Examined*, Lutterworth Press, 1979, p. 32.

Max Weber, *Economy and Society*, 3 vols.
Bedminster Press, 1968; *On Charisma
and Institution Building*, Chicago
University Press, 1968.

E. Käsemann, *New Testament Questions
of Today*, SCM Press/Fortress Press,
1969, p. 241.

Chapter Three

Th. Zahn, *Introduction to the New
Testament*, vol. 1, T. & T.
Clark/Scribner, 1909.

E. Lohmeyer, 'Die Offenbarung des
Johannes 1920–1934', in *Theologische
Rundschau* 6 (1934) 269–314, and
7 (1935) 2–62.

Chapter Four

E. Käsemann, *The Testament of Jesus*,
SCM Press/Fortress Press, 1968.

R. Bultmann, *The Johannine Epistles*,
Fortress Press, 1973.

Other books on the early church

There are not many other books which cover exactly the same material as we have dealt with here. The shorter New Testament books have not been extensively considered in recent literature, though naturally most series of commentaries include them.

General

J. A. T. Robinson, *Redating the New Testament*, SCM Press/Westminster Press, 1976. A provocative and radical examination of the dates given to the New Testament books. Has an especially lucid explanation of the problems involved, as well as new proposals.

F. F. Bruce, *Men and Movements in the Primitive Church*, Paternoster Press, 1979

(*Peter, Stephen, James and John*, Eerdmans, 1980). A brief, readable account of the life and work of selected personalities in the early church.

A. J. Malherbe, *Social Aspects of Early Christianity*, Louisiana State University Press, 1977. An important book exploring the way the early church fitted into Roman society.

R. M. Grant, *Early Christianity and Society*, Collins, 1978/Harper & Row, 1977. Examines the relationship of the early Christians to various aspects of lif in the Roman Empire.

G. B. Caird, *The Apostolic Age*, Duckworth, 1955.

J. D. G. Dunn, *Unity and Diversity in the New Testament*, SCM Press/Westminster Press, 1977.

Chapter One. Confronting the ancient world

John Drane, *Jesus and the four Gospels*, Lion Publishing/Harper & Row, 1979.

John Drane, *Paul*, Lion Publishing, 1976/Harper & Row, 1977.

M. H. Scharlemann, *Stephen: a singular saint*, Pontifical Biblical Institute, 1968. A scholarly book, but well worth making the effort to read.

L. E. Elliott-Binns, *Galilean Christianity*, SCM Press/Allenson, 1956. A helpful examination of what can be known about the early churches in Galilee.

M. Hengel, *Acts and the History of Earliest Christianity*, SCM Press, 1980. A helpful examination of the nature of the book of Acts, by an eminent German theologian.

F. F. Bruce, *The Speeches in the Acts of the Apostles*, Tyndale Press, 1942. Discusses the question of the authenticity of Luke's account of the speeches of early Christian preachers.

F. J. Foakes-Jackson and K. Lake, *The Beginnings of Christianity, Part I, The Acts of the Apostles*, Macmillan, 1942. A massive five-volume work dealing with all the issues involved in understanding Acts. A little dated now, but still a source of vast learning.

I. H. Marshall, *The Acts of the Apostles*, Tyndale Press/Eerdmans, 1980. A useful smaller commentary on Acts, with helpful notes on all the major problems.

Chapter Two. The Spirit and the letter

J. D. G. Dunn, *Jesus and the Spirit*, SCM Press/Westminster Press, 1975. A most helpful discussion of the charismatic nature of the life of the early church.

H. von Campenhausen, *Tradition and Life in the church*, Collins/Fortress Press, 1968.

E. Käsemann, *Essays on New Testament Themes*, SCM Press, 1963; *New Testament Questions of Today*, SCM Press/Fortress Press, 1969. Two collections of essays expounding

Käsemann's distinctive insights on the nature of early Christianity. Hard going but stimulating.

R. M. Grant, *The Formation of the New Testament*, Hutchinson/Harper & Row, 1965. Traces the history of the New Testament canon.